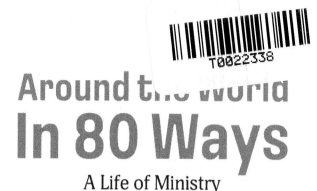

Around the World

In 80 Ways

A Life of Ministry

David Coffey

malcolm down

PUBLISHING

First published 2023 by Malcolm Down Publishing Ltd.
www.malcolmdown.co.uk

27 26 25 24 23   7 6 5 4 3 2 1

The right of David Coffey to be identified as the author of this
work has been asserted by him in accordance with the Copyright, Designs and
Patents Act 1988.

British Library Cataloguing in Publication Data
A catalogue record for this book is available from the British Library.

ISBN 978-1-915046-70-3

Cover design by Angela Selfe
Art direction by Sarah Grace

Printed in the UK

Commendations

Wisdom seems to be scarce these days. David Coffey writes as a seasoned fellow traveller and Christ-follower, and the result is a treasure trove of wisdom you won't want to miss. Practical, authentic and inspirational, David's heart and experience will stir and encourage you in your trek with Jesus. Highly recommended.

Jeff Lucas
Author, speaker, broadcaster

I have known David Coffey for over thirty years. I respect him as a church leader, pastor and man of God. I have been a part of a prayer group with him for several years, and I love him as a brother in Christ. You will find what he has written – whether for his grandchildren or the Church generally – a legacy that will be encouraging and honouring to God.

R.T. Kendall
Former pastor of Westminster Chapel, London

David's memoir is a legacy to his family and us, the Emerging Leaders Network of the Baptist World Alliance (BWA). When he served as the President of the BWA (2005-2010), he intentionally sought ways and means to bring in young leaders from different world regions and prepare them to take up the mantle of leadership. I highly recommend this book as an inspiration to parents and grandparents to invest in the lives of their children and grandchildren. It is also a must-read for ministers as an encouragement to multiply the impact of their ministry by mentoring young leaders.

Rachael Tan
Dean of Student Affairs, Taiwan Baptist Christian Seminary
Associate Dean, Asia Baptist Graduate Theological
Seminary, Taiwan

David Coffey is a world leader with a pastoral heart. I have always been amazed at his talent to navigate some of the most controversial global issues with a keen eye for seeking God's will and direction. Still, more than that, I have been inspired by his ability to do so while remaining amazingly accessible to everyone. Whether you serve in a local school or the head of the United Nations, he cares for you and seeks to help you understand what God wants to do in our life. His teaching, preaching, and counselling have inspired thousands worldwide, and I know it has profoundly impacted my life beyond words.

Adam Wright
President, Dallas Baptist University, Texas.

Many people in David Coffey's position and with his experience might be expected to write an autobiography. What stories he would have to tell, what secrets he might spill! Instead, David has chosen a better path. While not without biographical insights, David has put together a collection of sermons, addresses and reflections which express his convictions. Rooted in the gospel, expressed in his engaging and arresting style, and with disarming honesty, they reveal what has motivated him throughout his life. They provide a true foundation for future generations to follow. They also offer an excellent model for present-day preachers to emulate. This is a book to treasure and a book to savour. It cannot be read hurriedly but digested slowly to gain from its wisdom. And what a feast it will prove to be.

Derek Tidball
Former principal of the London School of Theology

Although primarily written for his grandchildren and wider family, these reflections on a life of ministry are a rich collection of biblical insights that provide a memorable memoir. I much enjoyed reading it, not simply because David is my brother and friend, but for the humble wisdom shared in its pages.

Ian Coffey (the younger brother)
Former acting principal, Moorlands College.

When I think about leaders who have shaped me most, David is at the top of that list. In *Around the World in 80 Ways*, he does it again. Drawing upon ministry in more than eighty countries, this will be a lasting legacy that once again equips us with a fresh leadership perspective, a call to deepen our love with the Lord, and a path to follow on the journey to wisdom.

Elijah Brown
General secretary and CEO of the Baptist World Alliance, Washington DC.

David's reflections on his ministry and life are a treat; they inspire devotion to following Jesus, encourage faith and show the richness of life in Christ. David reflects with humility and grace on the people he has met, and the privileges he has had, and does not dwell unhelpfully on the challenges or lament the failures of so many. This is a smorgasbord of insights into David's discipleship and years of leadership. His broad interests in music, sport and reading; his enthusiasm for life are thought-provoking and encourage the reader to make the most of their every moment. This is a highly readable book of personal reflections – he is more honest about his weaknesses and hardly mentions those of others.

Dianne Tidball
Past president of the Baptist Union of Great Britain

David Coffey has a beautiful way with words – whether from his mouth or his computer keyboard. With so many years of travel and preaching opportunity, having visited eighty countries on six continents, his collection of writings provides a welcome and rich resource – not only for his grandchildren but for all of us who continue to evaluate the transient earthly experience in the light of timeless Biblical Truth.

Dave Pope
Chief executive of Flame Trust

David's book is a *tour de force* of his local, national and international ministries and includes some of his most memorable sermons! The whole Church owes him a debt of gratitude, and it's an honour to be his friend.

Lyndon Bowring
Executive chair of CARE, London.

David Coffey never ceases to amaze me for the prolific preacher he is, who has an impressive ability to communicate with each person in their language. With King Abdallah of Jordan, I have witnessed him talking using the language of a decision-maker and pastor with a godly authority. With children, it was the same; he spoke their language, football language, and they eagerly engaged with him! His life is an inspirational journey that reveals God's grace and goodness. He is a remarkable pastor whose love for Jesus Christ radiated wherever he went.

Nabil Costa
CEO of LSESD, Lebanon
General secretary for the Association of Evangelical Schools, Lebanon

In the nearly 20 years I have known David as a dear friend and mentor, I have come to find a global pastor who is personal beyond all else, and his sermons, talks, and writings all point to this unique ability to engage, inspire, and ultimately point back to the beauty of God's Word and the incredible sacrifice of God's Son. His ministry has blessed and continues to bless my life, and I know it will also bless you.

Blake Killingsworth
Vice president for communications, Dallas Baptist University, Texas

Contents

Contents

Articles

Epilogue

Foreword

God has blessed my wife, Janet, and me with two wonderful children, Niki and Phil, and four amazing grandchildren, Sam, Abi, Nay and Bex. In the year I am writing this book, our grandchildren's ages range from twenty-one to twenty-seven.

When they were children, we would enjoy what came to be called red-letter days.

We have bulging albums of photographs which record these special days.

- The changing of the guard at Buckingham Palace.
- Christmas pantomimes in Oxford.
- Inaugurating the Dandelion and Burdock Club on Wittenham Clumps.
- T20 cricket matches in Worcester.
- Rugby matches in the rain at Banbury.
- Touring Stamford Bridge, the home of Chelsea FC.
- Monkey World in Dorset.
- The Roald Dahl Museum in Great Missenden.

- Ten pin bowling in Banbury.
- Punting on the River Cherwell.
- Late night evenings with the Marldon Movie Club.
- Summer barbecues by the Garden Lodge, here in our home in Devon.
- Breakfast on the beach at Broadsands.
- Singing those mad songs (not recently!), 'My Doughnut Lies Over the Ocean' and 'On Top of Old Smoky'.

Just a few selections from our albums of red-letter days.

Janet and I can now see that these special days were when the seeds of friendship were sown – so that each grandchild is now also a friend. We have prayed for our grandchildren since they were born (and before!) and over recent years have enjoyed the privilege of attending their baptismal services when they professed their faith in Jesus, and publicly professed a desire to be his lifelong disciples. Our daughter, Niki, and her husband, Peter, have been faithful parents to our grandchildren, the Ridgway gang. They have taught the Bible in the home and enabled the Scriptures to be seen in action by the quality of their own discipleship – a pattern of homelife which Paul discerned in the life of his young friend Timothy (2 Timothy 3:14-17).

When I celebrated my eightieth birthday in 2021, I decided I wanted to add to these fun-filled red-letter days and compose a book which would be a spiritual legacy to our grandchildren. Psalm 78 says the truths of God's Word we hear from our parents must be passed to the next generation, so that they know 'the praiseworthy deeds of the LORD, his power, and the wonders he has done' (Psalm 78:4).

I have the greatest fulfilment in preaching God's Word and sharing the Scriptures, so this book combines some of the sermons I have preached, addresses I have delivered and articles I have written. Before each chapter I indicate the occasion associated with the event.

I began my ministry as a pastor of local churches. I was then privileged to be called to be a 'tramp preacher', nationally and internationally. I have ministered in over eighty countries in six of the seven continents, hence the title: *Around the World in 80 Ways*.

I dedicate this book to my grandchildren and pass to them a saying given to me when I was twenty-one:

'Be absolutely his.'

The Ridgway Gang of Four

(bios supplied by the team captain, Sam)

Sam (twenty-seven) is head of marketing and Corporate Social Responsibility coordinator (CSR) for an Oxford-based law firm. He studied at King's College London where he captained the First XV Rugby Team. While studying for a Master's in criminology at Oxford, he played rugby for the Blues. He is married to Katie, a history teacher and talented worship leader, and they are members of St Aldates Church, Oxford.

Abi (twenty-five) after leaving school, spent six months working as an au pair in New Zealand before commencing her studies at Reading University where she was a member of the Christian Union (CU). She has just concluded a Master's in sociology at Green Templeton College, Oxford. Fiercely independent, she's not afraid to live outside her comfort zone and has the ability to befriend anyone she meets.

Nay (twenty-three) graduated from Oxford Brookes University with a first-class English degree.

During her student days she was on the committee of Just Love, an organisation which exists to inspire and release every Christian student to pursue the biblical call to social justice. She is the entertainer in the family and a constant source of wit and humour, balancing this perfectly with a caring and discerning heart. She works for an Oxfordshire landscaping and garden design company.

Bex (twenty-one) is in her second year reading history at Exeter University. She is a star baker and is frequently told she would make a great contestant for *The Great British Bake Off*!

In her vacations she can be found working in a Cotswold village café (serving the likes of footballer David Beckham) or browsing vintage shops for a stylish steal. Bex is the 'sensible' member of the gang, keeping Sam grounded while oozing coolness and class.

Left to right: Nay, Niki, Sam, Katie, Peter, Abi and Bex

Testimony to Generational Faith

I was ten when my mother, Elsie, took me to King's Cross station in London and sat me in the railway carriage beside the guard's van. I was travelling on the world-famous *Flying Scotsman*, the first steam train to reach 100mph. My mother asked the guard to look after me and ensure I left the train at Newcastle, where my uncle Ronnie would be waiting to meet me. She knew I was enthralled with steam engines and might be tempted to travel on to the final destination of Edinburgh.

Understanding why I was heading north to Newcastle requires sharing some of my family histories.

I am proud of my Irish ancestry. The surname, Coffey, is an Anglicised form of the Gaelic surname O'Cobhthaigh. The O'Coffeys in medieval times were found in Galway, Roscommon and Westmeath. They were famous as a bardic family in the latter county, with Diarmaid O'Coffey remembered as a sixteenth-century poet. Charles Coffey was an eighteenth-century playwright and actor who introduced Irish tunes into his operas.

The family of my grandfather, Thomas Coffey, were among the 2 million Irish people who emigrated to

Liverpool in the mid-1800s. In 1851, 20 per cent of the population of Liverpool was of Irish descent. They were escaping harsh economic conditions to find employment in the flourishing English labour market.

Thomas married my grandmother, Ada Foden, in 1900. They had seven children and lived in a 'two up two down' house at 90 Leadenhall Street, Everton, Liverpool. My father was the youngest in the family, born in 1914, two days after the outbreak of the First World War. Grandfather Thomas joined the King's Royal Rifle Corps in 1915 and died at the Battle of the Somme on 12 July 1916. My grandmother, Ada, received a war pension, but to support her family of seven children under thirteen, she took in washing for business people and charged 2s6d each load, 12p in modern currency. The eldest children collected and delivered the washing in a big basket – but always exited their house by the back alley so no one would see them.

My father was always preaching as a small boy. When he was four, he would put the cat on the garden wall and preach to it. The next-door neighbours used to say: 'That Arthur will end up with religious mania.' But instead, he ended up as a Baptist minister!

When my father was twenty-two, his mother died in a tragic accident. She had been to visit her daughter, Lily, in another part of Liverpool. She left at 10p.m. to get a tram home and, crossing the road, she ran in front of a tram and died instantly. She was just fifty-six. My dad lost his father when he was two, and then his mother's tragic death left him with unresolved grief for many years.

My dad gave his life to Christ during an evangelistic mission in Liverpool conducted by the Australian Methodist, Lionel Fletcher. Baptist minister Edwin Orr called Fletcher 'the outstanding evangelist between the two world wars.'[1] My father, with his friends linked to Richmond Baptist Church, acquired the use of disused shop premises where they held Sunday afternoon services. Will Stewart, a family friend and a contemporary of my dad, once told me he remembered my father as a gifted 'boy preacher'. He had moved on from preaching to cats to winning people to Christ!

Older believers in the Richmond church encouraged my father to train for Christian ministry, and he commenced as a student at All Nations Bible College.[2]

It was founded in London in 1892 as a missionary training centre and had a rich history of preparing men for global pioneering missionary work. In 1923 they established the college premises at Beulah Hill, not far from Spurgeon's College on South Norwood Hill. The first principal was the celebrated Bible scholar and preacher, F. B. Meyer. The main aim of the college was to provide a grounding in a knowledge of the Bible while developing the Christian character of a student. Street evangelism was a central part of its training. How would a student cope with preaching in China if they hadn't learned to share the gospel in London? During the 1930s, student friendships formed between All Nations and Spurgeon's College, where my father first met George Beasley-Murray. Thirty years later, George was my college principal when I commenced my studies at Spurgeon's.

I never knew either of my paternal grandparents. My father rarely spoke about his childhood days or mentioned his siblings. Although I had seven aunts and uncles on the Coffey side, I only knew my aunty Ivy, the eldest in the

---

1. Edwin Orr article 'Evangelistic Movements' in Ralph G Turnbull *'Bakers Dictionary of Practical Theology'* (London: Marshall Morgan and Scott, 1968) p. 161.
2. Now All Nations Christian College.

family. She was a tremendous Christian believer, softly spoken and gentle in nature. She and my uncle Ted were kind and generous and I always looked forward to their visits to our family home in Bournemouth. Aunty Ivy outlived all her siblings and died aged ninety-five in 1997.

My maternal family tree is also traced to Ireland. My mother, Elsie Maud Willis, was born on 10 February 1913, the seventh of nine children born to Joshua and Mary Willis. My grandfather, Joshua Willis, was born in Blackwatertown, County Armagh, on 21 May 1875. My grandmother, Mary Millar, was born in the village of Tamnamore near Dungannon, County Tyrone, on 7 November 1878. Her father was a master thatcher and farmer, and Mary was raised on a farm a short distance from the farm where Joshua was employed.

Joshua married Mary on 16 July 1901. Soon after, they moved to Consett, County Durham, where the Consett Iron Company employed my grandfather and, in time, rose to the position of blast furnace foreman.

I knew each of my eight uncles and aunts personally, in the batting order: Robert, John, Annie, Herbert, Norman, Norah, Ronnie and Margaret. The family's youngest member, Margaret, was born eight years after my uncle Ronnie. My mother was very close to her youngest sister and would mischievously say: 'Margaret was probably a mistake, but in those days, we were all mistakes!' All my cousins were very special to me and, to this day, I keep in touch with several of them, including the Australian branch of the Willis family, known as the Bolloms of Oz.

I never knew my grandfather, Joshua, as he died of cancer in 1932, aged fifty-seven, leaving my widowed grandmother with a family of nine children. But I've always felt I knew him because my grandmother and mother told me endless stories of his life, memorably the day of his conversion in November 1912.

It was grandad's routine to visit a pub on Consett marketplace on a Friday night, and one evening when he was leaving the pub, a Salvation Army Band was conducting an open-air service. He stopped to listen and heard someone read this scripture from Joshua 24:14-15:

Now fear the Lord and serve him with all faithfulness. Throw away the gods your forefathers worshipped beyond the river and in Egypt, and serve the Lord. But if serving the Lord seems undesirable to you, then choose for yourselves this day whom you will serve, whether the gods your ancestors served beyond the Euphrates, or the gods of the Amorites, in whose land you are living. But as for me and my household, we will serve the Lord.

Grandad Joshua was convicted by the plain speaking of Scripture. He heard the call to 'choose for yourself this day whom you will serve', and he responded by affirming, 'as for me and my household, we will serve the LORD'.

The Salvation Army officer who had read the Scriptures knelt in the market square, prayed with my grandad, and encouraged him to tell someone at work what had happened. He chose to tell two blast furnace supervisors who were local Brethren Assembly members. They responded, 'Joshua, we have been praying for you to come to know Jesus!'

Around the same time, my grandmother committed her life to Christ while attending a meeting conducted by evangelists from the Faith Mission. This Scottish charity was founded in 1886 by John George Govan for evangelism in the rural areas of Great Britain and the Republic of Ireland. My grandparents simultaneously experienced a spiritual renewal to fulfil Joshua Willis' promise in Consett marketplace: 'As for me and my house, we will serve the LORD.'

Movingly, my mother, Elsie, was born in February 1913, three months after her parents committed to following Christ. She was the first child in the Willis family not to be christened. Following the tradition of the Brethren chapel they were now attending, they said, 'We have dedicated Elsie to the Lord; that is enough.' On Sundays, my mother would be introduced to the Scriptures. On weekdays she attended Consett Church of England School with its pattern of daily prayers.

I can't recall my mother recounting one significant moment when she gave her life to Christ. I think this is because her whole life was a constant surrendering to the will of God. When she was thirteen, she recalled her father asking her whether God wanted her to be a missionary. She told me she felt my grandad was claiming for her life all the years he had missed being a committed Christian.

She had nurtured a dream from her childhood that she wanted to be a children's nurse. When friends called at the home to invite her out to play, my grandma would say, 'You will find Elsie at the house where they are expecting a baby.' She would share with her mother that she planned to have lots of children, at least seven or eight. Grandma Willis would pass the comment: 'What about finding a husband first?' Elsie replied: 'I don't need a husband!'

Whatever fanciful dreams she had as a child, God's call to be a nurse was stirring in her young heart. He used her Sunday school teacher, Jenny Cox, to confirm this calling. Jenny put her hand on my mother's shoulder one day and told her she had a special gift for working with children and that she should train as a nurse. Jenny would respond to God's call and sail to China in the 1930s, where she served as a missionary.

My mother was eighteen when she left Consett to travel to London (on the *Flying Scotsman*!) to work at the Mission of Hope in Croydon. In the 1930s, it was a social stigma for a young single woman to become pregnant. One of the options was for a woman to leave home and move to a city miles away where the baby would be born and then offered for adoption. The Mission of Hope was a Christian charity which offered a caring environment for a single woman and her new-born baby.

After three years, the matron identified that my mother needed a nursing qualification. She gained a place at St Giles' Hospital Camberwell and commenced her studies to become a State Registered Nurse (SRN).

One of the great love stories of the Old Testament is the relationship between Ruth and Boaz. In Ruth 2, her mother-in-law sends Ruth to work in the fields where they are harvesting. There is that deceptively simple phrase in verse 3, 'As it turned out', Ruth began working in fields belonging to the wealthy farmer, Boaz. The rest of the story is a beautiful unfolding of God's providence in the long story of salvation.

'As it turned out', the young nurse from Consett began attending the same church as the young Bible college student from Liverpool. In the 1930s, Rye Lane Chapel in Peckham was one of the largest Baptist churches in south London, with a membership of more than 1,000.

Theo Bamber was the pastor who ministered there for thirty-five years. His outstanding Bible teaching ministry attracted large numbers of students. Rye Lane had many families who exercised the gift of hospitality, and it was in these homes over Sunday suppers that the friendship between my mum and dad grew. A burgeoning romance eventually led to their engagement.

My dad finished his studies and was called in 1940 to the pastorate at Woodmansterne Baptist Church near Purley. My mother concluded her nursing training, qualifying as an SRN. They were married in February 1941, and I was born in November of the same year. My brother, Ian, was born ten years later, so never ask him if he is older or younger than me!

After four years in Woodmansterne, my parents would serve in two other pastorates, Winton Bournemouth (1944-55) and Chadwell Heath Essex (1965-1980). In addition, my father worked as deputation secretary for the North Africa Mission (1955-65).

When my parents celebrated their fortieth year in ministry in 1980, my brother, Ian, and I planned a surprise, *This is Your Life*, at All Souls, Langham Place. It was an inspiring occasion filled with stories of appreciation from friends they had known through the years. Four years later, in January 1984, my dear dad died aged sixty-nine. He had preached twice at Rugby Road Church, Worthing, and walked home to enjoy Sunday supper with my mother but sustained a massive heart attack and went home to be with the Lord. He died wearing his preaching shoes.

I thank the Lord for the immense privilege of being born into this Christian family.

The Coffey/Willis home was the spiritual cradle that shaped my life. It was a *home of hospitality*, and I recall a host of my parents' friends who befriended me and became honorary aunts and uncles. Anyone who has listened to my sermons will remember the famous Aunty Nellie!

It was a *home of laughter*. My dad was a scouser, and though he had no taste for football or any sport, he had the most exquisite sense of humour, which my brother, Ian, and I have inherited.

It was a *home of generosity*. Both my parents had experienced hardship and grief in their early years, which gave them hearts of compassion and generosity for the broken-hearted.

It was a *home of discipleship* where I observed what it meant to 'grow in the grace and knowledge of our Lord and Saviour Jesus Christ' (2 Peter 3:18). My parents were regular attenders at the Keswick Convention, hosting an annual house party which Janet and I attended from the late 1950s. Listening to various gifted Bible teachers deepened my faith and shaped my later ministry of Bible exposition. But the most significant influence on our family life was the spiritual legacy of the 1930s East African revival, which had spread to many parts of the world. The UK annual conferences took place in Abergele, Clevedon and Southwold. These were led by Roy Hession and a team of ministers and missionaries whose lives had been touched by this Holy Spirit-led revival.

Strong links were forged with those who had experienced the revival first-hand; Jo Church and William Nagenda were regular participants at the annual conference, which we attended as a family. With its scriptural emphasis on repentance and grace, transparent fellowship and walking in the light with other believers, these annual gatherings were always heart-warming occasions with many times of refreshing from the Lord. Roy Hession was a gifted Bible teacher and a personal friend. He and his wife, Pam, moved to Torquay in his retirement, and I had the privilege of being their pastor.

It was a *home of persevering love.* I observed at a close hand how my parents worked hard at their marriage. I have already shared how my dear dad lived for years with unresolved grief and, as a result, suffered from severe bouts of depression. In his early forties, he had a major breakdown in health and had to leave the pastoral ministry and receive residential care for a season. I recall my mother saying that God had given her a verse of scripture which she claimed as a promise:

I have seen [his] ways, but I will heal [him];
I will guide [him] and restore comfort [to him] . . .
(Isaiah 57:18)

This promise was gradually fulfilled, and through the years my dad's health improved, and it was beautiful to see the loving companionship my parents enjoyed in their retirement years.

They were both very active in their local church in Worthing. Robert Brown was a close friend of my dad and they had worked together for the North African Mission. Robert Brown paid this tribute to my dad at the time of his funeral:

We shall miss Arthur's wise counsel, his almost card index memory for names,
but above all for his joy and humour. If Arthur was present, there was joy.
He was transparent in his love and dedication to the Lord Jesus Christ.

Sometime during the early 1980s, Janet and I attended the Keswick Convention, and Stuart Briscoe gave the

Bible studies based on the Ten Commandments. I recall being deeply challenged by his exposition of the fifth commandment: 'Honour your father and your mother, so that you may live long in the land the LORD your God is giving you' (Exodus 20:12).

I came away from Keswick determined to send my mum and dad a letter honouring them for all they had meant to me: their unconditional love, numerous sacrifices and constant prayers.

I didn't keep a copy of the letter I wrote to them. But when my mum died aged ninety-three in May 2006, I went through her possessions and found a similar note I had sent to her on her ninetieth birthday. Here are some of the things I shared:

As I get older, I have become more reflective, and I am deeply aware that I want to emulate your best qualities in my life. These are some of the things I admire in your life:

You have a great love for people.

You are a peacemaker by nature.

Your capacity for generosity and friendship is why so many people seek you out for wise counsel.

Your prayer life has been a consistent example of how to be a follower of Jesus in all four seasons of the spirit.

You are rarely judgemental (most of the time), and this explains why I am so well-adjusted (most of the time).

You can laugh at yourself (and there is a lot to chuckle about).

You have the gift of plain speaking – salty speech seasoned with affection.

You are a natural evangelist. One day in heaven, a crowd of people will be queuing up to say, 'Thank you,

Elsie, for introducing me to Jesus', and I will be at the front of the queue!

You have never forgotten your working-class roots and the plight of people living in hardship and poverty.

You have the gift of encouragement par excellence. You taught me that once you believe in God, you can believe in yourself because the Lord works within you to will and do his good pleasure.

Thanks for being a wonderful mum to Ian and me. For opening your heart to include my beloved wife Janet – to whom you were a mother. Then my fantastic children Niki and Phil, my wonderful son-in-law Peter, and my beautiful grandchildren Samuel, Abigail, Naomi and Rebekah.

Who would have guessed God's excellent plan for our family on 13 November 1941?

Postscript for Sam, Abi, Nay and Bex:

Grandma and I know you have been incredibly blessed by the privilege of living in a Christian home. You have experienced generational faith. Now let this blessing be passed through you to a further generation, who will follow in the steps of your great, great grandfather Joshua Willis, who knelt and prayed in Consett Market Place in November 1912:

But as for me and my house
We will serve the Lord.

Arthur and Elsie Coffey

Family celebration for my eightieth birthday

Sermons

In October 2021 I was invited by my good friend Dave Pope to give some Bible studies at the Timeout holiday conference and decided to take the theme of 'Reimagining the Future' with studies on Matthew 24-25; this talk was part of the series.

The annual conference is a gathering of friends who are prayer partners of the Christian charity Flame Trust which supports school academies, disadvantaged people, mentoring and social development.

I have had the privilege of speaking at a number of these gatherings, including the beautiful islands of Madeira. I have always been inspired by the rich fellowship of Timeout guests and their eagerness to study God's Word.

1

The Burglar, the Butler
and the Bridesmaids

Matthew 24:1-51; 25:1-13

It is said that faith in Jesus Christ without believing he will return to earth in triumph, is like a flight of stairs going nowhere and a book without a final chapter. Central to the Christian faith is the Easter confession:

Christ has died:
Christ is risen:
Christ will come again.

You will remember that Jesus said to his disciples that they would see him return to earth 'with great power and glory' (Mark 13:26) What did Jesus teach about his return? How do we wait for the return of Christ? What signs are there that Christ will return? What are the responsibilities of the waiting Church?

Matthew chapters 24 and 25 enables us to consider the teaching of Jesus on his return to earth. The chapters open with the disciples admiring the beautiful Temple buildings which had been dedicated to the glory of God. Such was the magnificent beauty of the Temple, it was considered indestructible. Jesus repudiates this thinking and invites his disciples to ponder the unthinkable. All these magnificent stones will be destroyed (v. 2).

When they arrived at the Mount of Olives, not surprisingly, the big question posed by the disciples was to privately enquire of Jesus if they could be given a sign of what happens at 'the end of the age?' (v. 3). The rest of chapter 24 is Jesus' answer to the question.

At first sight the chapter is full of complex verses. Some refer to immediate events which will happen within forty years; some refer to long-term events with no timeline, and some indicate there will be one final event before the second coming of King Jesus. The challenge is they overlap and intertwine. Only a careful study of the structure of the verses determines the interpretation of the passage.

Here is the big picture. The whole chapter is primarily about the end of all history. We are living now in the Last Days. At the beginning of his ministry, Jesus announced the arrival of the kingdom of God (Mark 1:14-15), and since his death and resurrection, his ascension to heaven and the sending of the Holy Spirit at Pentecost, his kingdom has been secretly growing on earth, and his Church is one of the significant signs of the kingdom.

We are God's kingdom citizens demonstrating the values of the kingdom. One day Jesus will return to wind everything up and usher in his kingdom. He will come in glory as the King and on that day every eye will see him. Meanwhile we are to keep our eyes on the King who is returning to be crowned!

Jesus speaks of 'birth pangs' (v. 8, RSV) which will precede his return and the predicted fall of Jerusalem (vv. 16-21) is an extremely painful example of a 'birth pang'. The language of birth pains in Old Testament and Jewish thought is used when God is bringing something new to birth in his world. Prior to its birth there will be labour pains of tribulation.

These pains point to an inevitable outcome – the birth of a new creation. The birth pains signal clearly the coming of a new age. A new creation has been conceived, it is growing in the womb, but is yet to be born.

Jesus is describing the whole period between his first coming and his return to earth.

As the beginning of the 'birth-pains' (v. 8), the kingdom of God arrives in the person and ministry of Jesus, and this kingdom for the past 2,000 years has been secretly growing and the expansion of the global Church has taken place. In this waiting period before the King returns, we must expect there will be birth pains.

Painful things that indicate God's kingdom is coming in its fullness. This means when we observe in our country the growth of a bold atheism; the appearance of increasing ungodliness; the famine of Bible knowledge; a disrespect for the Christian faith in the media; Christians in the workplace losing their jobs for taking a conscience stand for their faith in Jesus; the harrowing persecution of believers worldwide – these are all deeply troubling birth pains which have to be endured.

The disciples asked their significant question in *turbulent days* (v. 2) when Jesus warned unthinkable things were about to happen to the social fabric of their world. The disciples could not imagine a world without the Jerusalem Temple. It was imposing and looked as if it was built to last forever, but Jesus predicted the destruction of the Temple in Jerusalem.

These were days of *spiritual confusion* (v.4) which is why Jesus said to his disciples, 'See that no one leads you astray' (ESV). Every generation of the Church has experienced seasons of spiritual confusion, and we are not to be deceived by the religious confusion of our own day:

- Moral confusion around sexuality self-designation and the transgender debate;
- Spiritual confusion about whether the Bible is the final authority on matters of faith;
- Leadership confusion with countless moral failures of high-profile church leaders.

These were *dangerous days* for the disciples of Jesus (v. 6) and Jesus issues several warnings about impending wars and 'rumours of wars'. Jesus said that nation would 'rise against nation' (v. 7), and the fact is they still do. Currently there are ten major conflict zones in the world[3] to which we can add the ongoing dangers in the United Kingdom with unseen terrorists and their random acts of terrorism.

Jesus predicted terrible *days of persecution* for his followers (v. 9). They would be 'put to death' and 'hated by all nations'. Some believers would renege on their faith and betray and hate each other. False prophets would emerge to deceive God's people. I have just read Terence Ascott's book, *Dare to Believe!* It is a compelling story of the suffering Church standing firm while the world collapses into anarchy and chaos. It is action-packed with powerful

---

3. www.crisisgroup.org (accessed 10.5.23).

testimonies of dramatic conversions to Christ and a hunger for Christian fellowship and Bible teaching. There are vivid stories of persecution, intimidation, blood-soaked martyrdoms and miraculous escapes.[4]

Jesus warned of such dangerous days when:

Believers are arrested
Churches are firebombed
Thousands disappear without trace
Christians dying hideous deaths.

Then the chilling warning, there will be days when 'the love of *most* will grow cold (v. 12, my italics).

We are like the first disciples. We live in turbulent days, in spiritually confusing times, in a dangerous and unpredictable world where there is extreme persecution for believers. All of us know how the love of believers can grow cold.

So how will we endure, and how shall we live as we wait for the return of the King?

First, the *gospel* must *be preached* throughout the whole world (v. 14). Even in turbulent confusing and dangerous times, we are to go on preaching the gospel to all nations.

Second, we are to *avoid date fixing* (v. 3 6). In view of the plain statement of Jesus about avoiding date fixing, it is incredible that believers should be obsessed with it. No one has God's diary.

Our task is to '*keep watch*' (v. 42, my italics) as we await the return of the Lord Jesus Christ. All Christians should be looking and longing for the second coming of Christ which will be personal, visible, glorious and final

---

4. Terence Ascott, *Dare to Believe* (Searcy, AR: Resource Publications, 2021).

(Acts 1:11; Revelation 1:7; Mark 13:26; John 5:21-29; Hebrews 9:27-28).

Jesus then tells three memorable parables on how we can remain vigilant.

1. The burglar teaches us to be vigilant (vv. 43-44)

A small parable about a burglar was a shaping influence on Paul, Peter and John, and they used this image in their writings:

> The day of the Lord will come like a thief in the night . . . But you . . . are not in darkness so that this day should surprise you like a thief.
> *(1 Thessalonians 5:2,4)*

> But the day of the Lord will come like a thief . . . Since everything will be destroyed in this way, what kind of people ought you to be? You ought to live holy and godly lives . . .
> *(2 Peter 3:10-11)*

Jesus says to the church at Sardis which had a reputation for being alive, but was dead:

> Remember, therefore, what you have received and heard; hold it fast, and repent. But if you do not wake up, I will come like a thief, and you will not know at what time I will come to you.
> *(Revelation 3:3)*

The mark of the thief is he comes without warning. It's a surprise! My coming, said Jesus, will be without warning.

We are to be vigilant because the world *won't* be vigilant. In the day of Noah people were eating, drinking and getting married. These people were not evil, but there was no vigilance in their lives. They were not looking for God at work in his world. They were oblivious to the flood of judgement (v. 37).

In the twenty-first century, God is not building a physical ark but a community of people. He is building a people of power who are anticipating the return of King Jesus. Every Sunday you can hear the hammers and nails on construction sites in thousands of places. This is the sound of God building his people of power. Faithful disciples who have chosen to build their lives on the solid rock of Jesus Christ.

Michael Green has said that Christians are to watch for the second coming of Christ:

Not like astronomers through a telescope, or guards watching a CCTV screen, but like lovers who can't wait for another glimpse of the beloved, or captives in a labour camp longing for the day that will allow them home[5]

We are the vigilant ones, always ready for the unexpected.

2. The butler reminds us to be reliable (vv. 45-51)

Jesus then told the story of two butlers; the first servant is faithful and reliable. The master of the house may not be physically present in the house, but the butler serves as if the master is present. Do you see yourself as a servant who serves faithfully while the master is absent?

---

5. Michael Green, *The Message of Matthew* (Leicester: IVP, 2000), p. 259.

In your daily life and witness
Your generous giving to the Lord's work
Your ministry to neighbours and strangers
Your practice of hospitality
Serving daily doing ordinary duties?

Jesus told another parable about a servant who had a hard day working in the fields (Luke 17:7-10). He posed the question, would the master invite his hardworking servant to put his feet up and have supper? 'No,' said Jesus! The master would more likely say to the servant, 'Prepare my supper and wait on me while I eat, and after that you may have your supper.' Jesus then added, 'Can you imagine the master thanking the servant for doing what he was expected to do?' It appears a harsh parable, but it is the reminder from Jesus that when we have done everything expected of us, we simply say: 'We are unworthy servants; we have only done our duty' (Luke 17:10). He is the Master, and we are the servants, and our encouragement is his words: 'Blessed is that servant who is working for me when I return' (see Matthew 24:46).

Charles Haddon Spurgeon was the pastor of the 5,000-member church at the Metropolitan Tabernacle in London. One day he was interviewing a young woman who was applying for church membership. She worked as a servant girl in one of the large south London houses. Spurgeon asked her how she served the Lord and what difference had Jesus made in her life. The girl thought for a moment, and then replied: 'I don't lift the carpet and brush the dust underneath!' She was faithful in her duties when no one was looking.[6]

---

6. Attributed to C.H. Spurgeon. Source unknown.

Look at the disgraceful behaviour of the second butler (vv. 48-49):

He treats the other servants roughly.
There is his lack of self-discipline.
He eats and drinks with the town drunks.

What is so startling about this picture is Jesus is describing the family of God. The previous verses referred to the faith of Noah and his worldly generation, but this is life in the Church.

This unreliable servant seems to ignore the values of his master's home and provides a dreadful example of how not to serve while waiting for the master to return. One of the distinguishing marks of Christians in the time of waiting is how we behave towards other family members.

There is a solemn moment in the parable when the master returns and the life of the unworthy servant is cut to ribbons. He suffers endless torment.

The parables of Jesus are not a final comment on our lives when we know we have failed as servants. Jesus is not undermining your eternal assurance of life with him for ever. But he *does* challenge our complacency. This parable is a warning so we can amend our ways. It is an invitation to look at ourselves in the mirror of Scripture:

Do I really want to be an unreliable servant?
Ending my life with deep regrets and isolated misery?
Or do I strive to be a reliable and faithful servant
Who receives the 'well done' of his master?

3. The bridesmaids remind us to be prepared (25:1-13)

In Bible days Middle Eastern weddings were long and joyful occasions and could last for two weeks. There was no set time for the bridegroom to arrive at the bride's house where there would be a lavish wedding feast.

The bridegroom would then take the bride to his house where the marriage celebrations could last for days. The role of the bridesmaids was to escort the bridegroom when he arrived at the home of the bride, and they would go out to meet him (v. 1). Because of the unpredictable timetable, the bridesmaids could be kept waiting for hours.

In the parable, there is a long delay waiting for the bridegroom to arrive (v. 5) and the guests (aided by the drink!) become drowsy and fall asleep. It was possible for the bridegroom to arrive in the dark hours around midnight when lamps were required to light the way to the home of the bride. Oil was needed to keep the lamps burning, which would require rags dipped in oil and carried on a stick waiting to be lit.

The sleepy guests are suddenly wakened by the midnight shout, 'Here's the bridegroom!' (v. 6) and everyone goes out to meet him, led by the bridesmaids. The five wise bridesmaids were ready and prepared with their lamps, they had dipped rags in oil waiting to be lit. The five foolish bridesmaids were caught napping and had forgotten to have their lamps prepared. They begged their wise colleagues, 'Please, give us some of your oil!' But there was no time to rush to the supplier of oil – even if they were open at midnight!

The bridegroom and his escort were greeted by a depleted retinue of five bridesmaids who lead the wedding party into the house and then the door is slammed shut!

The remaining bridesmaids return with their newly purchased supply of oil, but it is too late. They plead to be admitted to the wedding celebrations, but the man on the door says he doesn't even recognise them and sends them away. The door was shut and there was no possibility of access. Jesus ends his story with the solemn words: 'Therefore keep watch, because you do not know the day or the hour' (v. 13).

At the commencement of the story, all ten bridesmaids outwardly looked the same – but inwardly there was a big difference. Five were wisely prepared and five were careless in their preparation. When the critical moment arrived, the ill-prepared five pleaded to their companions to lend them what they had forgotten to bring.

This observation could be made of any gathering of Christians. Outwardly, we may look similar as we join in acts of worship and enjoy fellowship after a service. But whatever the similarities, in some hearts there can be a foolish attitude which imagines we can borrow the faith of other believers.

There are some things that cannot be borrowed in the Christian life:

You can't borrow Christian character.
You can't borrow years of Christian service.
You can't hope that others will shine a light for you.

The foolish bridesmaids may have thought their light would not be missed, but it was.

They may have thought one missing light won't make a difference, but it does.

Everyone needs to shine their light for the darkness to be banished.

Do see yourself in this parable as one of the foolish bridesmaids? The Lord's intention is not to make you feel guilty, but he *is* seeking repentance and reform. But what message of hope is there for the lost years? At this moment you may be living a life full of regrets, pondering seriously how you might retrieve the lost years when you failed to serve the Lord wholeheartedly. There is a great promise of hope in the God's word: 'I will repay you for the years the locusts have eaten' (Joel 2:25).

Colin Smith exercises a very fruitful Bible teaching ministry through his radio programme *Open the Bible.* He describes the true impact of the locust years we can't retrieve: 'They are fruitless years, painful years, selfish years and above all, Christless years.'[7] Ask anyone who came to faith in Jesus Christ later in life, and they will share that they wish they had become a follower of Jesus sooner than they did. How can we experience the promise of God that lost locust years can be restored?

First you *deepen your relationship with the Lord* and begin right now by saying to him:

Lord, I confess the locust years have been fruitless, painful, selfish, rebellious and Christless years:

I have blamed everything on people and circumstances.
I have buried the past refusing to acknowledge my failure.
I have done everything in my own strength.
I humbly draw near to you right now.
I ask for your forgiveness and cleansing.
Please restore to me the lost years.

---

7. Colin Smith, 'God Can Restore Your Lost Years', article 18 July 2014, www.thegospelcoalition.org (accessed 24.4.23).

Second, you *live with the hope of fruitfulness*. By faith you begin to live believing that God *will* restore those lost years by making the rest of your life abundantly fruitful. In the 1970s when I was pastoring a church in North Cheam, Surrey, we had the joy of seeing a very wealthy couple in their late fifties come to faith in Christ. They lived in a magnificent house on the edge of Epsom Downs, and after they surrendered their lives to the Lord their house, which had previously been a home for two, became a haven for hundreds as they discovered God's gift of lavish hospitality.

In another church we had an interesting discovery in our offering. On a monthly basis a brown envelope would be deposited with a large amount of bank notes and written on the envelope were the words 'back tithe'. Someone had realised the lost years had been lived selfishly and they were now repaying to the Lord money they owed from the locust years. Do you believe the Lord can restore to you the years the locusts have eaten? Let me offer this prayer for you based on the words of Isaiah 61:1-3:

Lord, please bestow on my life today a crown of beauty instead of a pile of ashes.
I want the oil of gladness instead of a constant mourning over the past.
Please clothe me with garments of praise instead of a spirit of despair.
I repent and return to you.
In your pity, I ask you
to pour out fresh gifts of grace into my life
and grant me years of abundant harvests of blessing.

In January 2021, when I was planning to celebrate my eightieth birthday in the November, I decided to take a sabbatical from preaching and teaching.

I made a short list of holy habits for each weekday. First, to be in my study by 8.30a.m. Second, to leave my iPhone and iPad outside the study so I would be free from distractions. Third, to compose a daily prayer based on verses from the Gospels.

To stimulate the composing of the daily prayer, I decided to commence reading the three volumes of Meditations on the Gospel According to Saint Matthew *by Erasmo Leiva-Merikakis,[8] a Trappist monk at St Joseph's Abbey in Spencer, Massachusetts.*

The following two chapters are talks based on Matthew 5:1-12.

I have often chosen this Bible passage for conferences where I am speaking.

In particular I thank the following groups for the fellowship I enjoyed at their conferences as we looked at Jesus' teaching from the Sermon on the Mount: Belmont Chapel Exeter, the Scottish Baptist Lay Preachers, the Methodist Evangelicals South West, the South Eastern Baptist Ministers and Church Leaders, and the Southern Counties Baptist Leaders.

---

8. Erasmo Leiva-Merikakis, *Meditations on the Gospel According to Saint Matthew* (San Francisco, CA: Ignatius Press, 1996).

2

The Character of the Disciple

Matthew 5:1-6

There is a simplicity about the opening words of Matthew 5: 'Jesus . . . went up on a mountainside and sat down. His disciples came to him, and he began to teach them' (v. 1).

It's what we are doing as we read these opening verses to the Sermon on the Mount. We are approaching Jesus and allowing him to be our teacher. Jesus begins his teaching with a comprehensive portrait of a disciple. The eight Beatitudes of Matthew 5 are considered the jewel in the crown of Jesus' teaching and can been termed eight beautiful attitudes.

Each one of the eight is prefaced with the word 'blessed' which is sometimes translated as 'happy', but this word is a mistranslation as Jesus is not addressing how we feel, rather what God thinks of us. When we display these attitudes in our lives then we are blessed by God, and we receive his favour.

The first four beatitudes concern the character of the disciple. Our poverty of spirit; expressing sorrow for our sins; a true reality about who we are; and an insatiable hunger and thirst for the living God.

In the next chapter we look at the remaining four beatitudes. They describe how the disciple lives in an alien culture. We practise being merciful in a merciless world; our purity of heart enables us to follow Jesus with a single mind; we are committed to peacemaking in a world at war; we are willing to count the cost of discipleship and shed blood for our faith in Jesus.

Let us examine each beatitude in detail.

1. Spiritual poverty is coming to an end of my own resources.

'Blessed are the poor in spirit, for theirs is the kingdom of heaven' (v3).

The phrase 'poor in spirit' has a long history in the Old Testament, especially in the psalms, where it describes those who have confidence in God alone. Whenever the psalmist is burdened by a long-standing personal distress or lament for the plight of the nation, the cry from the depths is: 'In God alone I trust.'

King David exemplifies this disposition of poverty of spirit as he contemplates the numerous blessings God has bestowed on his life and exclaims: 'Who am I, O Lord GOD, and what is my house that You have brought me this far?' (2 Samuel 7:18, MEV).

There is a biblical commitment to support the materially poor, and this was central to Jesus' ministry, and it belongs to our gospel calling. But verse 3 is describing 'the poor in spirit'.

The first beatitude invites rich and poor to acknowledge an utter dependence on God.

We have no power in ourselves to enrich our own lives. Our first awareness as disciples is the poverty of our resources and the abundant supply which is found in God. The poor in spirit are those who know their spiritual need, who realise they cannot survive without help from outside. As Kent Hughes says: 'Blessed are those who are so desperately poor in their spiritual resources that they realise they must have help from outside sources. Poverty of Spirit, then, is the personal acknowledgement of spiritual bankruptcy.'[9]

In my early days as a pastor, I practised a theology of the well. That is, I saw myself as a pastoral well supplying others with the water of life. It was a very simple principle. Needy people would come to me, and I would supply their spiritual requests:

I was the wisdom in their house of ignorance.
I was the calmness in the eye of their storms.
I was the pillar of strength for their family.
I was 24/7 available for their needs.

It was a simple principle, but it was wrong, and if I had continued with this theology of the well, spiritually I would have died and pastorally I would have perished.

The theological deficiency of the well is one day people lower the bucket into your well, and instead of the sound of the splash of water, all you hear is the death rattle of a bucket banging on the side walls of an empty well.

Too frequently in my life I have failed to heed the words of Jesus, that without him I can do nothing, but with him all things become possible (John 15:5). A bucket rattling on

---

9. R. Kent Hughes, *The Sermon on the Mount* (Wheaton, IL: Crossway, 2001), p. 17.

the side of an empty well is a haunting sound. I can recall numerous times leading a team of gifted people facing mountains of perplexity. Those moments in meetings when no amount of enthusiastic energy and creative ideas can break the logjam, and there is a weary emptiness in the hearts of experienced leaders.

Sometimes it was when church members failed to see what we perceived as a God-given vision; often it was the yawning gulf between our faith aspirations and the stark reality of our finances; there were those hollow moments when a serious moral failure had shamed the church family and stunned the wider community, and the media were demanding an immediate statement; there was always the recurring ailment in the healthiest of teams, the fear of people instead of the fear of the Lord. These moments of emptiness are where wisdom begins.

Frank Viola suggest that while emptiness is difficult, it is beautiful because it makes God look great. Our gifts draw attention to us; emptiness draws attention to God.[10]

It is worth remembering that spiritual emptiness brings its rewards. There is a blessing in possessing nothing. Each of the beatitudes carries a promise, and to the poor in spirit Jesus says, 'You have the kingdom of heaven.' What is most striking about this promise is the present tense, whereas by contrast other beatitudes are a future tense promise. The text says unequivocally the kingdom belongs to the poor in spirit, which means they are on a parity with the King himself.

We are the recipients of the generosity of Jesus Christ. He was rich but became poor for our sake. He did this that 'through his poverty' we might be enriched (2 Corinthians

---

10. Frank Viola *God's favourite place on earth* (Colorado Springs, CO: David C. Cook, 2013).

8:9). The true blessing of spiritual poverty is when I able to affirm that I have come to the end of my own resources, and I am daily depending on an endless supply of gifts from the King who enriches my royal life.

2. Sorrow is accepting responsibility for my spiritual condition

'Blessed are those who mourn, for they will be comforted' (v. 4).

This verse promises the comfort of God as a timely consolation in time of bereavement. When our loved ones have died, then we can cling to this promise of being comforted by the Lord. He will draw alongside us as the divine consoler. When the cares of our heart are many, then his consolations cheer our soul (Psalm 94:19).

But the context of this verse is not mourning for my loved one who has died; it is grieving over the person I am. It is the sorrow of repentance for falling short of being a faithful citizen of the kingdom. It is weeping over the sins of others and mourning for the depth of suffering created by sin. This kind of mourning is in the tradition of the Old Testament prophets like Jeremiah, known as the weeping prophet, who expressed an overwhelming mourning for the plight of his nation:

Oh, that ... my eyes [were] a fountain of tears! I would weep day and night for the slain of my people.
(Jeremiah 9:1)

My eyes will weep bitterly, overflowing with tears, because the LORD's flock will be taken captive.
(Jeremiah 13:17)

Some object to this practice of lament and find it morbid and mediaeval. They say, 'Where is the joy of the Christian life?' As someone once said to me on this verse, 'I ceased to grovel as a Christian the day I left my sins at Calvary.'

But there *are* times for self-examination when we repent and mourn over our spiritual condition. Erasmo Leiva-Merikakis speaks of the simple act of the disciple being with Jesus as the normal condition of the disciple. In order to fix our eyes on Jesus, we must constantly nourish our minds in the scriptures. 'The revealed Word of God has set Christ Jesus before us in order that we may have that on which we fix our eyes.'[11]

It is enriching to meditate on this verse on mourning and ask the Holy Spirit to turn this into a prayer. When I pray, I list the things in my life over which I mourn:

- I mourn for everything in my life which had failed to reflect Jesus and his life-affirming grace.
- I mourn for my wasted musical gift.
- I mourn for my lack of discipline in the study.
- I mourn for my impurity and lust in thought, word and deed.
- I mourn for the years I had failed to pray consistently for people in my care.
- I mourn for my manipulative ways ensuring my version of events are in the headlines.

When I mourn for my spiritual condition, the accompanying promise is: 'You will be comforted', so we call on the divine

---

11. Erasmo Leiva-Merikakis, *Fire of Mercy-Heart of the Word*, Volume 3 (San Francisco, CA: Ignatius Press 1996), p. 34.

comforter to come with his cleansing power to renew and transform us from within.

3. Meekness is my willingness to be real before God.

'Blessed are the meek, for they will inherit the earth' (v. 5). We need to remember who is teaching us. Jesus portrays each of the beatitudes in his own life. The one who said, 'Blessed are the meek' also said 'I am meek and lowly in heart' (Matthew 11:29, MEV). Jesus invites his followers to follow his example of being gentle, humble and considerate. He laid to one side the privileges of heaven and bowed his will to God's loving purposes.

This is the humility of God's servant. There is no place for showtime pride in the kingdom. Just look at the King!

The secret of becoming a child of the King is to be yoked to him and learn the furrows of discipleship from the Master. It is known that often in ancient farming, an experienced animal would be yoked with a less experienced one. Just as two cattle are yoked together to perform one task – so I must willingly wear the yoke of obedience with the one experienced in doing what most pleases the Father.

But this is costly. To demonstrate weakness seems too passive and timid. It takes courage to be meek as it involves patient waiting. The psalms often mentions those who are meek of heart and how they will inherit the land and enjoy great peace (Psalm 37:11). The worshippers singing these psalms were either living in a land they didn't possess, or because of evil people they had been deprived of their possessions. So, what could they do? With meek hearts they had to trust and wait for God to act on their behalf. They were meek in heart and believed in the promise of God's word as they sang the words:

Wait for the LORD, and keep to his way, and he will exalt you to possess the land; you will look on the destruction of the wicked.
(Psalm 37:34, NRSVA)

I can think of numerous occasions where I failed to display this disposition of waiting on God in meekness. Trust and wait were not part of my discipleship vocabulary. In my early years of leadership, I justly earned the title of 'Instant Coffey'!

I modelled myself on characters who led boisterously from the front. I was loud and proud and full of urgent ideas and actions to solve the problem of the hour. In those moments meekness of spirit deserted me, and I had my own version of this beatitude: 'Blessed are the bold of heart for they will win.' My thought processes were governed by action man principles:

- I must be seen to be the leader.
- I can't lose this decision, or the church will think me weak.
- If I admit I'm in the wrong, it will be a sign of weakness.
- I must appear as the omnicompetent one, as this is the mark of a true leader.

In my early days as a leader, where I really lacked meekness was when I felt threatened by gifted people in my team. I practised teamwork, but with one proviso – I had to be the most gifted member in the team. I can recall in one church taking a summer vacation, and I delegated the task of preaching and pastoring for almost five weeks to two of my gifted elders, a biochemist and a cancer consultant.

When I returned to the church in September, I met a couple in the church car park who greeted me with an unusual enthusiasm. 'David,' they exclaimed, 'we have just enjoyed the most amazing month of ministry while you have been away. We have had top-rate Bible teaching for the past month and the pastoral care has been amazing. Welcome back!'

I would like to say that I instantly recalled the words of John Bunyan:

He that is down needs fear no fall
he that is low, no pride;
he that is humble ever shall
have God to be his guide.[12]

But at that stage of my life, I had never read Bunyan's helpful saying. But I had read the spiritual check-up advice of W.E. Sangster, where he asks the question:

Do I want God's cause to advance, or is it my chief desire that I should advance it?[13]

It's a tough moment to distinguish these two options and always opt for the first. My default non-meek position is a strong desire to personally advance the kingdom. That summer I learned some painful lessons in leadership. First, I am entirely dispensable. I am valued and appreciated for who I am and the work I do, but life goes on when I am not around. Sometimes, life is richer when others step up

12. John Bunyan (1628-88), hymn, 'He That is Down Needs Fear No Fall', https://hymnary.org/text/he_that_is_down_needs_fear_no_fall (accessed 10.5.23).
13. Jennifer Atkinson and Robin Mark, adaptation of William E. Sangster's 1952 Westminster Pamphlet (Milton Keynes: Authentic Publishing, 1991).

to make their contribution. Second, I don't have to be the most gifted member of a team, even if I am leading it. Third, there are times when things often work better if I am not involved. People are not required to work according to my fixed agenda and my way of doing things. Fourth, I must be open to team members challenging me. So, when I claim a particular task is in my job description, the team can respond by saying, 'It may be in your job description, but is this really your responsibility on this occasion? Is there a person better suited to carry out this piece of ministry?'

After many years of ministry, I hope I am coming near to the true meaning of meekness.

Meekness is never a loss:

- It is a blessing with a promise of inheritance.
- It is having a true estimate of myself.
- It is willing to be small in order for the Lord to be magnified.
- It is bending the neck to let God do things his way.

In the words of the Wycliffe Bible translation of this verse: 'Blessed be mild men . . . for they shall wield the earth.'

4. Spiritual hunger is seeing Jesus as the answer to all my needs

'Blessed are those who hunger and thirst for righteousness, for they will be filled' (v. 6).

It is a natural law that hunger prompts us to eat in order to maintain our energy levels, and thirst is the cue we need to drink to prevent dehydration of the body. I have never fasted and prayed for forty days, and never gone on hunger strike as a civil protest about an injustice.

It is a spiritual law that hunger and thirst need to be satisfied. Spiritually, it is natural to desire consistently those things that please God. It is unnatural in spiritual terms not to be hungry. The poet F.W. Faber suggests: 'for the lack of desire is the ill of all ills'[14]. In Luke's version of the beatitudes, Jesus follows the blessing of hungering and thirsting for righteousness with a stern warning: 'Woe to you who are well fed now, for you will go hungry' (Luke 6:25).

Any disciple of Jesus who becomes content with life as it is and lacks any desire for the righteousness of God to flow freely in their lives, needs to ask the Lord for a great awakening in the heart. Jesus knows that our hunger is aroused by the right spiritual climate, which is why there is a logical progression as he teaches the first three beatitudes.

- Spiritual poverty is coming to the end of my own resources.
- Sorrow is accepting personal responsibility for the condition of my life.
- Meekness is a willingness to be yoked to Jesus and learn from him.
- Hunger and thirsting is seeing Jesus as the answer to all my needs.

If all spiritual life is fired by longing, then Jesus desires to create in us a desperate hunger and a burning thirst for

14. F.W. Faber (1814-63), 'Desire of God', www.traditionalmusic.co.uk-fabers-hymns (accessed 10.5.23).

a vital relationship of obedience and trust in God. The accompanying promise is that this passionate longing will be ultimately satisfied. David knew something of this deep spiritual longing which he reveals in his prayer song:

You . . . are my God, earnestly I seek you;
my soul thirsts for you.
my body longs for you
in a dry and weary land where there is no water.
(Psalm 63:1, NIV 1984)

When I first became a Christian as a young teenager, I didn't know much about hungering for God, although I had plenty of physical wants and desires. I confess this was a season in my early Christian life when a hunger and desire for righteousness had yet to take root in my life. But a turning point came when I attended the Keswick Convention in 1959 and listened to some great Bible teaching. But by the middle of the week, I was full to the brim with spiritual food. It felt like the spiritual equivalent of being served steak and chips followed by sticky toffee pudding three times a day and I couldn't eat another thing.

But the strange thing was that I was spiritually hungry. This was a desire, not for more Bible knowledge, but rather a profound hunger and thirst to find out what God was calling me to do for him. It was the kind of deep longing that through the years I have experienced repeatedly, but this was the first awakening. I was eighteen and the whole of my life stretched ahead of me. I had commenced a career in local government with Surrey County Council but there was a growing sense that the career direction was about to change. This was probably the first time in my life when I was truly hungry and thirsty for God and his righteousness. There was an all-consuming hunger that God would reveal himself to me.

When everyone left the house for the meetings of the day, I decided to stay behind and go to my bedroom. I can remember getting down on my knees and opening my Bible and reading Isaiah 42. I know the only one who perfectly fulfilled this servant song of Isaiah 42 is Jesus the Messiah. But the Lord spoke to me as I read verses 6 and 7:

I, the LORD, have called you in righteousness;
I will take hold of your hand.
I will keep you and will make you
to be a covenant for the people
and a light for the Gentiles,
to open eyes that are blind,
to free captives from prison
and to release from the dungeon those who sit
in darkness.

I was hungering to discover God's will for my life, and in that moment, he answered my prayer. The Lord didn't reveal the specific details of the rest of my life that morning, but I heard clearly the call of God on a Wednesday in July 1959 in No. 42 Eskin Street, Keswick. Later that week I stood at the missionary service and publicly surrendered my life for Christian service. After sixty-four years of serving the Lord, that hungry week is still vivid in my mind.

What does Jesus intend with this focus on hungering and thirsting 'for righteousness'?

Righteousness is a rich Bible word and can mean:

Enjoying right relations with God;
Possessing the right character of a disciple;

Living in right relationships in community;
Longing for restorative justice in the wider world.

This means I begin by hungering to be right with God, and by faith in the death of Jesus he freely provides me with the gift of justification. I then progress as a disciple by hungering for my character to grow in grace and goodness, and by the indwelling power of the Holy Spirit the process of sanctification gradually shapes me into the likeness of Christ. But I am not destined to be a loner as God has placed me into his family of followers, and in the life of a local church community. This is where I learn to hunger for the blessings of fellowship with other disciples. But a disciple is never satisfied with just meeting personal needs or enjoying the blessings of life in the Christian community, there is a never-ending hunger and thirst for the kingdom of righteousness to come in God's world. As my good friend Philip Greenslade says:

And tasting the presence of the kingdom of saving justice stirs up a whirlwind of desire for God's new order of things, an aching appetite for God's empire of freedom rather than Rome's empire of oppression, a craving for a compassionate justice that restores God's true covenant community among us. Who is there who has tasted the grace and power of God's gracious kingdom, who does not look out on our fractured and dysfunctional world and not hunger and thirst for such a righteousness.[15]

---

15. Philip Greenslade, *Voice From the Hills: Costly Grace/Crucial Words* (Surrey: CWR, 2008), p. 25.

Jesus promises to those who hunger and thirst that they will be filled, and so we can pray:

Jesus, the joy of loving hearts
the fount of life, the light of men;
from the best bliss that earth imparts
we turn unfilled to thee again.
We taste of you, the living bread,
and long to feast upon you still;
we drink of you, the fountain head,
our thirsty souls from you to fill.[16]

---

16. Latin, twelfth century translated by Ray Palmer (1808-87), *Baptist Praise and Worship* (Oxford University Press 1991).

3

Discipleship in an Alien Culture

Matthew 5:7-12

We have seen how the first four beatitudes concern the character of the disciple, our disposition towards God. The remaining four depict our attitude as we face outwards to the world. This is how to be disciples in an alien culture. We practise being merciful in a merciless world; our purity of heart is singleness of mind in following Jesus; we are committed to peacemaking in a world at war; we are willing to count the cost of discipleship and suffer for our faith.

1. I show mercy because God is merciful to me.

'Blessed are the merciful, for they shall be shown mercy' (v. 7).

Mercy is not a natural disposition. It is a gift that grows and develops as we remember how much God has forgiven us. I show mercy to others because God has been merciful to me.

Jesus in the Sermon on the Mount constantly repeats the same message. The only way to become merciful is to remember the reciprocal practice of mercy at the heart of the Lord's Prayer:

'Forgive us our sins, as we forgive those who have sinned against us' (see 6:12)
'If you forgive, then your heavenly Father will forgive you' (see 6:14)
'If you don't forgive, then your heavenly Father won't forgive you' (see 6:15)

Withholding forgiveness from those who harm us is not the way of mercy. Without mercy in our heart, we allow grudges to grow like ivy around a wall. These bitter grudges cling to us and can take over our lives. Where an unforgiving spirit takes root:

- It can divide happy families.
- It can split fruitful churches.
- It can break successful businesses.

Mercy is the antidote to the misery of grudges. We develop this beautiful attitude of mercy by remembering how much God has forgiven us. I show mercy because God has been merciful to me. Those who have tasted God's mercy show mercy to others.

In the life and ministry of Jesus we see mercy in action. It is not simply forgiving those who have wronged us, it is love in action to anyone in need. It is more than feeling compassion but doing something positive towards alleviating physical need. This quality of mercy is revealed in the parable of the Good Samaritan (Luke 10:25-37). When Jesus was asked the question, 'Who is my neighbour?' by an expert in Jewish law, he replied by telling the story of the man who was mugged and robbed and left half-dead by the roadside.

Three people had the opportunity to come to the assistance of the man who had had been mugged. Two religious people saw the man and chose to pass by on the other side of the road. The third man was the most unlikely to help. He was a Samaritan and his race steered clear of Jewish people. Jews considered Samaritans the least respected of people and they were to be avoided at all costs. But this despised person proved to be an amazing friend to the man who had been robbed and left for dead.

While others scurried past, this man hovered over the man who needed aid. Jesus describes in detail the compassionate actions of the Good Samaritan:

- He takes pity on the man.
- He bandages his wounds.
- He puts oil on the wounds to sooth his pain and wine to disinfect the cuts and bruises.
- He puts the man on his own donkey and walks alongside.
- He takes him to an inn and stays overnight to ensure the man is recovering.
- Before he leaves the inn, he gives two silver coins to the innkeeper, sufficient for twenty-four days.
- He asks the innkeeper to look after the injured man, and indicates he plans to return and reimburse the innkeeper for any extra expenses incurred.
- He meets the physical and economic needs of a man who has been mugged.

The Samaritan did everything he could to be a good neighbour to a total stranger. After he told the parable, Jesus asked his questioner: 'Which of the three people in the story proved a good neighbour to the man who had been mugged?'

> The expert in the law replied: 'The one who showed him mercy.'
> Jesus said, 'Go and do likewise.'
> *(vv. 36-37)*

This parable is the most significant lesson on the quality of mercy in the life of the disciple. Showing mercy to others – especially the stranger – is the strongest evidence you have received mercy from God. Mercy identifies with the miserable in their misery.

I recall visiting the city of Quito, the capital of Ecuador. Like many countries in South America, it is impossible to ignore the *ninos de la calle* – the street children of Quito. At all the major traffic junctions they approach your car selling newspapers or sweets. They sit on the pavements looking hungry and lost. My wife, Janet, and I were taken to a day school for children in one of the poorest parts of the city. The children in this school were the fortunate ones, as for many Ecuadorian children, school is never an option. Working parents can't afford to give them an education and basic childcare proves a challenge. While their parents work, children wander the streets begging for money.

We were introduced to the young woman leading the project for around 120 children. The children attended lessons, they were fed a substantial lunch, they had games and activities in the school playground. As you entered the school there was a large sign on the wall in Spanish:

Entrena a un nino en el camino que debe seguir Y cuando sea Viejo, no se aparatara de ella.

It is a verse from Proverbs 22:6 which, translated, says: 'Train up a child in the way he should go; even when he is old he will not depart from it' (ESV).

This Christian school with its clear purpose of caring for children began with the gift of mercy that God planted in the heart of a young woman in her late teens. She would walk home from work each day and her heart was touched by the plight of these hungry street children. She began by inviting one or two children to come home and share the evening meal with her family. Her father was a local pastor and he and his wife admired the commitment of their daughter in caring for the poor.

What began as a handful of children being fed at the family table grew after a few months to a dozen hungry children, so much so that the family had two sittings for supper. The pastor confessed to me that he began to wonder if his daughter's heart of mercy had become too heavy a burden for the family. The pastor was in touch with a group of American missionaries who admired the ministry of the young woman, and realised God had given her a vision beyond children being provided with an evening meal. They located a vacant building in the area and purchased it with a view to it becoming a day centre where children could be fed and cared for, taught basic education and learn the gospel stories and songs of the love of Jesus.

It was inspiring to visit the school and as we drove away to visit another project, our driver said to us: 'Do you know our nickname for this gifted young woman who leads the project? We call her the girlfriend of Jesus, because he chooses to share things with her that he doesn't share with anyone else. She is an inspiring example of God's mercy in action.'

2. Purity of heart is seeking first the King and his kingdom.

'Blessed are the pure in heart, for they will see God' (v. 8).

I know I am intricately made when I consider the functions of my physical heart. It is roughly the size of a normal fist and is located slightly to the left of the middle of my chest. It is the muscle that pumps around five litres of blood around my body. It sends oxygen and nutrients to all parts of my body and carries away unwanted waste products. But this awesome pumping station is not the Bible's meaning of the word 'heart'.

The heart that Jesus is referring to is our unique personality, which is the sum total of mind, emotions and will. The mind refers to our intellect; the emotions refer to our feelings; the will refers to our decision-making. All three in summary mean our heart. The very core of our being.

As a child in Sunday school, I was encouraged to give my heart to Jesus, and I learned songs to remind me of the importance of a whole-body commitment which included a loving heart:

Two little eyes to look to God.
Two little ears to hear his word.

Two little feet to walk in his ways.
Two little lips to sing his praise.
Two little hands to do his will.
And one little heart to love him still.[17]

I sang this song with little understanding of its full meaning; except I realised the heart was very important, and the older I became as a young disciple I realised the heart was the heart of the matter! As a mature disciple, I need to guard my heart.

If I am going to have a heart for God, then it has to be a totally pure heart. I need the cleansing from sin that Jesus gives me when I become a Christian, and I need a daily washing from sin to keep my heart pure. I need the conviction of faith that Christ is dwelling in my heart.

When Jesus was teaching these words, outward purity was the big thing. What you did outwardly was important, and it was vital that people observed what you were doing. On the street corner you offered long prayers, and in the worship place you ostentatiously gave generous gifts. It was obvious by your outward appearance when you were fasting. In prayer, giving and fasting, everyone saw your outward life and thought you must be very holy and devout.

Jesus challenged people for majoring on outward purity while ignoring the need for inner purity. Living like this was like cleaning the outside of a cup until it sparkled while ignoring the dirty stains on the inside of the cup (Matthew 23:25-26). The focus of outward purity is 'look at me'. The focus of inward purity says 'look at God'.

There has to be inward purity, and all my life I have battled to keep a pure heart. I have often used the prayer

17. Author unknown.

of David for the many moments when I have failed to keep a pure heart:

> Have mercy on me, O God,
> according to your unfailing love;
> according to your great compassion
> blot out my transgressions . . .
> Create in me a clean heart, O God,
> and renew a steadfast spirit in me
> *(Psalm 51:1,10)*

Purity of heart involves moral integrity. I need an exact correspondence between my inner and outer life so that what I believe and what I practise are one thing. The more I have studied and prayed over the Sermon on the Mount, the greater the realisation I have of the personal way Jesus speaks to me. There is his recurring phrase in Matthew 5 – 'I say to you'. It is an inescapably personal phrase and I know it is the authority of Jesus' words to the command centre in some key areas of living:

- Uncontrollable anger (5:22)
- Secret lust (5:28)
- Heart-breaking divorce (5:32)
- Careless swearing (5:34)
- Forgiving the enemy (5:39 and 44)

The key to radical inner purity of heart is having a single vision of God and what he wants. James 4:8 issues a call to a purity of heart for those who are 'double-minded'. Jesus says there are often two choices we will be faced with.

Two paths to journey; two gates by which we enter; two foundations on which to build; two ways to plough a field; two masters to follow. But double vision always impairs the ability to focus, which is why Jesus gives us the priority for purity of the heart: 'Seek first his kingdom and his righteousness' (Matthew 6:33).

Purity of heart is living with a single purpose. I seek first the King and his kingdom. In every situation I ask, 'What does God think and what does he want of me?' Serving one master you discover this truth, that when we put God first, all other things fall into their proper place.

3. I accept the call to be a peacemaker

'Blessed are the peacemakers, for they will be called children of God' (v9).

In the original Greek, the word 'peacemaker' is full of energy. It is not a passive but a dynamic word, which is a reminder of there being wrong ways of looking at peacemaking. We can think of it as a passive quality – some people will do anything to keep the peace. A true peacemaker is neither an avoider nor an appeaser. They don't avoid confronting difficult situations – they are not aiming for peace at any price. There is a time to confront issues and choosing the moment to bring everything out into the open. This is why peacemaking can be so painful.

When I reflect on the conflict situations I have experienced through the years, in the home with family relationships, in the church among the members of the community, in the workplace with other employees, I recall the times I have faced a choice of actions. Do I:

- Step in with conflict resolution?
- Keep the peace and don't rock the boat?
- Just let things take their course?
- Sense it's not my business to get involved?
- Recognise feelings are running high because nothing is being done?

Peacemaking is always pain-filled, and the challenge for the peacemaker is the willingness to become involved with pain-bearing:

- Initiating a chat with an estranged friend.
- Listening to people's anger.
- Risking failure and rejection.
- Striving to listen to all sides.

For several years, I was involved in international ministry and encountered numerous examples of courageous peacemaking by Christian disciples. I learned some of the principles and practices of the just peacemaking movement, a movement which has sought to develop a biblical theology for peacemaking based on the Sermon on the Mount. I have learned two important lessons (there are more than two!). First, you need a long and rugged commitment to be a peacemaker. Think years, not days. The second lesson in making peace is the need to acknowledge responsibility for any injustice and seek repentance and forgiveness, and the example I provide comes from South Africa.

Like many denominations in South Africa, Baptists were historically divided along racial, lingual and doctrinal grounds. Racism played a major role in the broken bridges.

This resulted in a major split in the 1980s, when three of the four associations withdrew from the Baptist Union of Southern Africa and formed separate associations. Much suffering resulted because of the division as disputes over property and pensions saw Baptists fighting and turning their backs on each other. But over a period of time God worked a miracle of healing and reconciliation, and central to this process was a meeting that took place in May 1998 in the small city of Colesberg in the Northern Cape Province of South Africa. My friends Terry Rae and Paul Msiza have shared with me the story of the historic meeting that took place in Colesberg.[18]

One hundred and eighty people had gathered, ninety representatives from each group. On the first day of the gathering, they were in small discussion groups in a large hall. The task of each group was to write down on a flip chart the grievances and hurts that had been caused by actions, statements and attitudes of the other group. Some groups kept coming back for more paper. These papers were then stuck to the wall of the hall.

They covered one wall from end to end and people were invited to walk silently down this passage of grief. Delegates from both groups were entering the process of reconciliation for the first time. Many of them wanted to leave the forum and go home. It was the first time some of them had expressed or heard the deep hurts caused by their division, and these experiences were still immensely painful.

After prevailing on everyone to remain and see the process through to the end, no one left.

The next day, after a restless night, the devotional time was centred on the cross of Jesus Christ. For a short while,

---

18. Notes from a document provided by Terry Rae and Gideon Makhanya.

the gathering looked away from their personal pain and focused upon the sufferings of Christ.

The two groups were seated on two sides of a hall. After twenty minutes of tense silence, one of the delegates rose to his feet and looked across at another delegate and confessed that he had criticised and spoken evil of his fellow Christian. He asked for forgiveness. The two men met each other in the aisle and embraced. This started a floodgate of confession and repentance, with scores of people from both sides standing to confess and asking for forgiveness. There was much weeping; there were little prayer groups all over the hall; there were black and white delegates hugging each other and repenting for their behaviour and attitudes of the past. This reconciliation went on for five hours without stopping.

Finally, exhausted, they took a brief break. During this time, the communion table was prepared. When they returned to the hall, the two groups sat at the Lord's table together for the first time since 1987. Terry Rae described how:

On the first day of the Colesburg meeting, a sheet of paper 120 feet long was filled with the misunderstandings and difficulties of the past years. After a time of admitting sins and receiving God's pardon around the Lord's Supper, the sheet was placed under the communion table. 'We placed it under the blood of Jesus Christ,' he said. 'After the communion we had a mandate from God to reconcile with each other.'[19]

The gathering declared that they would not resurrect the issues that were under the table, where they were covered by the blood of Jesus.

19. 'Reconciliation in South Africa', *Baptist World* magazine, October/December 1998, p. 10.

Ask the Lord what painfilled peacemaking work he is doing in the world and where he wants you to be involved.

4. I am prepared to suffer for Jesus (Matthew 5:10-12).

The final one is a double beatitude: 'Blessed are those who are persecuted because of righteousness, for theirs is the kingdom of heaven' (v. 10); Blessed are you when people insult you and persecute you and falsely say all kinds of evil against you because of me' (v. 11).

Suffering for the cause and the name of Jesus is inescapable. If you are not told this in your early days as a disciple, then you are being sold a deficit discipleship.

The great cause for which we will suffer is God's righteousness (v. 10). The great name which attracts suffering is the name of Jesus (v. 11). Following Jesus will unavoidably attract insults, persecution and all kinds of evil.

It's as if Jesus is saying, 'If you display in your life these eight beautiful attitudes there will be a price to pay.' If you choose to live a life dedicated to shaping everything towards God and his will, then you will stand out, and it's the conspicuous life that attracts persecution. Paul affirms when he says: 'Everyone who wants to live a godly life in Christ Jesus will be persecuted' (2 Timothy 3:12).

You need to note verse 11. It says blessed are you *when* people insult you not *if* they insult you. There are numerous references in the Gospels which carry the warning that the persecution of disciples will intensify as the end of time:

You will be handed over to be persecuted.
You will be put to death, hated by all nations because of me.

At that time many will turn away from their faith.
They will betray and hate each other.
Many false prophets will appear and deceive many
people.
(based on Matthew 24:9-11)

These words of Jesus have been fulfilled in every
generation of the Church. We may strive to live at peace
in this world and serve our neighbours with love and
compassion, but some people will not want to receive the
ministry of Christ through his people. As John Stott has
observed, persecution is the result of a clash between two
irreconcilable value systems, the value system of Christ the
King and the values of a godless world:

> The Sermon on the Mount is the most complete
> delineation anywhere in the New Testament of the
> Christian counterculture. Here is a Christian value
> system, ethical standard, religious devotion, attitude to
> money, ambition, lifestyle and network of relationships
> – all of which are totally at variance with those of the
> non-Christian world. And this Christian counterculture
> is the life of the Kingdom of God, a fully human life
> indeed but lived out under the divine rule.[20]

The first time I encountered the persecution that results
from the clash between two irreconcilable value systems
was when I visited the former USSR in 1986 as part of a
delegation of nineteen British and Irish church leaders.
Between 1956-64 under Nikita Khrushchev there had been
a planned intensification of persecution against the Church.

---

20. John Stott, *The Message of the Sermon on the Mount* (London: IVP, 1978), p. 19.

We were visiting a land of spiritual fruitfulness and terrible persecution, a place of deep darkness and oppression of Christian witness, but also a nation where the light of Christ was shining brightly in the lives of courageous believers. In 1960, the communist State had introduced new restrictive laws governing all churches. Among the new laws was when and where church services could be held, who was authorised to lead a church and preach sermons, a ban on teaching children and young people the Christian faith, and the most controversial law of all, churches had to register with the government. This blatant persecution divided the Baptist community. The majority of Baptist churches acted with discretion and registered their churches, not because they agreed with the new laws, but because they wanted to continue to exist as working communities of faith and believed they could find ways round the restrictive laws.

But hundreds of Baptist congregations, with courageous valour, refused to register their churches. They believed the State had no authority to legislate for the Church. Jesus was Lord and head of the Church, and they took their stand in proclaiming the crown rights of King Jesus and refused to register their congregations. The penalty for refusing to register a church was imprisonment, and by 1964 the number of pastors and church members who had been imprisoned by the government had grown to 197. The unregistered churches gathered information on all prisoners, including why they had been arrested and the length of their sentences. Their documents named the families of the prisoners, as children could suffer because the State refused to provide any financial support for the relatives of prisoners. They listed information on the Soviet prison camp system, including the exact location of many of the camps.[21]

By the year of our visit in May 1986, the plight of the prisoners and their families was well known in the West and prayers were regularly offered and protest letters were sent to the Soviet Embassy in London. In advance of the tightly managed itinerary, I had agreed with my friend Roy Jenkins that we would make a private visit to the family of Vladimir Zinchenko, a Baptist pastor who'd been imprisoned for failing to register his congregation. He had been sentenced in 1984 to three years in a strict regime Labour camp. His wife, Vera, had gained notoriety when she unfurled a banner outside Moscow's Baptist church, drawing attention to the religious persecution of pastors. This had happened during the visit of more than 200 Christians leaders from the United States.

The pastor was 3,000 miles away in a Siberian prison camp and Roy and I went to encourage his wife, Vera, and her two children. The family lived on the sixth floor of a depressing tower block in a district south of Moscow city centre. Without giving any notice, we climbed the stairs and knocked on the door of apartment No. 119.

We introduced ourselves to Vera, a young woman in her mid-thirties, and she invited us in, where we met her two children. She shared the story of how her husband, Vladimir, came to be arrested and with great pride expressed her strong support for the protest action he had taken. Instead of keeping a low profile, she continued to campaign for the release of Vladimir and when the authorities said, 'All Vladimir must do is agree to register your church then we will release him,' Vera responded vehemently: 'No way!'

---

21. Michael Bourdeaux, *One Word of Truth* (London: Darton, Longman & Todd, 2019), p. 117.

Vera had visited her husband in prison in February 1986, and in June 1985 had been able to take the children to visit their father. When we asked how she was coping financially with no support from the State, Vera said her neighbours were exceptionally kind and generous.

The conditions in the prison camp were harsh and she shared a letter from Vladimir which had been smuggled out of the camp. The camp authorities had attempted to persuade other prisoners to sexually attack Vladimir, but they had refused to cooperate as they believed Vladimir was a good man and didn't deserve to be serving a prison sentence as pastor. She shared news of the unregistered churches in the Moscow region and said that the editor of their magazine had recently been arrested and was awaiting a court trial.

Through the whole of our visit Vera portrayed herself as a woman strong in her faith, undaunted by the privations of having to support herself, supremely confident her husband was suffering for the name of Jesus. At the end of our meeting, Vera invited us to kneel on the floor of their small living room while she read from the Bible and prayed for us. As pastors we had gone to encourage her!

I walked away from the dingy tower block in Moscow knowing I had seen the eight beautiful beatitudes lived out before my eyes. This family was experiencing the blessing that Jesus promised to those who were persecuted because they were his disciples: 'Blessed are you when people insult you, persecute and falsely say all kinds of evil against you . . .' (v. 11).

In the following years I would encounter the same State persecution of the Church and gross infringements. On behalf of the Baptist World Alliance, I led delegations on Human Rights and Religious Liberty to Vietnam and China and I learned that every Christian must expect opposition.

You don't have to live under an oppressive regime to experience persecution. If you hunger for righteousness, then you will suffer for the righteousness you desire.

Notice the three types of persecution which are mentioned by Jesus:

- When people insult you and mock your faith and disparage your beliefs. The Greek word for 'insults' is the same word describing the insults hurled at Jesus on the cross.
- When people 'persecute you'. This means to run after someone in order to capture them. It is pursuing someone with the intention of harming them.
- When people 'falsely say all kinds of evil against you'. It has been observed there is an ascending progress of false accusations against Christians. First, there is disinformation when false things are shared; next there is denigration, when untrue things are widely disseminated, and finally, there is outright discrimination which is when character assassination occurs.

How are we to react to persecution? Not by retaliating. Not by self-pity. Not by toning down our faith. Jesus says we are to 'Rejoice and be glad' (v. 12). This is not the first thing you think of when you are being ridiculed for your faith in Jesus! But the joy of the believer has a unique quality. David Gill describes joy as an attitude of mind we adopt towards the challenges we are facing:

Joy is the mirth, the smile, the lightness and release of the spirit within us that emerges when we are able to (1) see with gratitude the good that is present (the glass that is half full!) and (2) to let go of the challenges we cannot meet and the problems we cannot fix (the glass is half empty).[22]

Why are we to be joyful when we are under attack for being a follower of Jesus?

First, because we are suffering 'because of righteousness' (v. 10). The Bible knows the pressures of living as a Christian surrounded by unrestrained behaviour, evil desires, drunkenness, orgies and lawless behaviour and explains the reaction towards believers who refuse to join the party: 'They think it strange that you do not plunge with them in the same flood of [wild living], and they [slander and] abuse . . . you' (1 Peter 4:3-4, NIV 1984).

If you aim to keep yourself sexually pure, then those who are sexually unrestrained will interpret your Christlike life as condemnation of their own lifestyle. If you fail to conform, prepare to be ridiculed.

But there a second reason to be joyful; we are suffering because of Jesus (v. 11). Jesus knows that if we go public in our love for him then we will suffer because we have chosen to follow him, and we need to see this a medal of honour, not shame. Take your stand for the exclusive claims of Christ the King on your life and it will be noticed. In the early days of the Church the apostles were arrested, physically beaten by the authorities and then released. Acts 5:41 says they left 'rejoicing because they had been counted worthy to suffer disgrace for the Name'.

But there is a third reason to be joyful when experiencing persecution; it means we are suffering in a great tradition

---

22. David W. Gill, *Becoming Good: Building Moral Character* (Westmont, IL: IVP, 2000), p. 199.

(v. 12). Many other believers have been persecuted before us. We only must read the roll call of honours described in Hebrews 11:

> Some faced jeers and flogging, and even chains and imprisonment. They were put to death by stoning, they were sawn in two; they were killed by the sword. They went about in sheepskins and goatskins, destitute, persecuted and mistreated – the world was not worthy of them. They wandered in deserts and mountains, living in caves and in holes in the ground. *(vv. 36-38)*

We need this message as never before. We may live in a society where religious freedom is valued and we are free to worship as we choose. In the face of the severe persecution experienced by many followers of Jesus, the challenges of living in a society where Christian faith is considered an outdated irrelevance does not constitute persecution. It only serves to demean the meaning of the word for those who are truly suffering for the faith. However, we must prepare ourselves for ongoing campaigns to change laws which have Christian foundations, and there is a growing need for believers to defend the Christian faith and be prepared to pay the price.

In 2015 I was heading to Israel and Palestine for some ministry visits and on the flight to Tel Aviv, I read the book by Tom Doyle, *Killing Christians*.[23] The stories he shared of believers meeting in secret, torture chambers in grim prisons, and bloody executions of those who had paid the ultimate price for publicly confessing Jesus as Lord, were

---

23. Tom Doyle, *Killing Christians* (Nashville, TN: Thomas Nelson, 2015).

deeply challenging and inspirational. A recurring theme of the book was the need for the Western Church to recover a theology of martyrdom. Instead of thinking of Christians dying over there, we need to remember it could be over here. It made me aware that I had to address the question whether I was willing to die for Jesus? How could I ever think that serving Christ would demand anything less than this kind of commitment.?

I sense that our baptismal vows need to be rewritten to profess that:

Jesus is Lord.
I promise to serve him for ever.
I am willing to suffer and die for Christ.

These eight beautiful attitudes are impossible to reproduce if they are separated from the one who first shared them with us. Jesus longs to share with us the power of his love.

Gracious Father,
I begin this sabbatical with you,
desiring it to be unique in the many Sabbath retreats I have had in your presence.
I meditate on this word *macarios* or blessed and realise that this is you looking at me.
I am blessed in your eyes as I make my prayer today.
You know the dispositions of this busy heart.
You know my fears and anxieties.
You know my fear that time is running out.
You know I no longer take for granted I will live to enjoy my eightieth birthday.
I am dependent upon you for life itself.
Every breath I take is a gift of your grace.

So, from this day forward, please increase the deep
longing, the yearning,
the panting of the soul for you the living God (Psalm 42:1).
If it is part of your perfect plan that I should complete
this book – this burden I possess to write a spiritual
legacy for my grandchildren and their generation –
then I present myself as 'poor in spirit' for your service.
I have no wisdom without you.
Without you there is no creativity, no motivation,
no organising of my material.
Without your aid I have no single-mindedness,
no memory of things learned,
and experiences gained.
Come, Holy Spirit, and call to my remembrance all
that will enrich the life of others.
I feel again a boundless, silent joy when I realise who
it is who is calling me.
A calling to the marvellous adventure that lies before me.
Grant me the spirit that understands
that only adventurous hearts are capable of following
Jesus intimately.

*This prayer was composed during my sabbatical on
Wednesday, 6 January 2021, based on 'Blessed are the poor
in spirit, for theirs is the kingdom of heaven' (Matthew 5:3).*

This sermon was preached on Sunday, 26 July 2009 at the European Baptist Federation Amsterdam400 Conference, celebrating the 400th anniversary of the founding of the Baptist movement. Baptists from around the world gathered in Amsterdam for a three-day celebration marking 400 years since the movement's founding.

It was in 1609 that John Smyth and Thomas Helwys left persecution in England in search of the freedom to worship God according to their conscience in Amsterdam. What started out as just a few committed followers meeting in the backroom of a bakery has grown over the centuries into a worldwide movement of more than 40 million members. The celebration explored the movement's historical beginnings and sought to discern God's calling on Baptists for the future in the areas of mission, community, freedom and discipleship.

As the president of the Baptist World Alliance, I was invited to preach at the celebration service. Smyth and Helwys are a powerful inspiration for Baptists in today's Europe where religious liberty is once again at risk.

The liberty of the Church to follow her Lord is under threat, and we must look now at how we were founded and what it is from our founding mothers and fathers we can take as an inspiration today.

4

Sent Like Jesus

Philippians 2:1-11

It has been inspiring to hear the story of our beginnings as a Baptist movement. We have particularly focused on the courage and vision of John Smyth and Thomas Helwys and their founding work here in Amsterdam. But each member body of the European Baptist Federation has spiritual pioneers whose lives we celebrate today. These visionary men and women brought to each of our nations a Baptist vision of a believers' Church which was also a missionary Church.

The 1609 founders of our movement believed they had been sent by Jesus Christ when they began a journey of discipleship with Jesus. The early Baptists followed in the footsteps of Jesus, and what a journey they made, full of costly adventures! We also have a journey to make which will be equally costly.

The early Anabaptists said there are three kinds of baptism. A baptism of the Spirit when by faith we are united to Christ; a baptism of water when we confess publicly our faith in Jesus Christ as Saviour and Lord, and a baptism of blood which is the daily dying to self. It is this latter baptism which is the genuine mark of the Christian disciple. As Jesus laid down his life in obedience to God's call, so we are called by God to be sent like Jesus, who said: 'As the Father sent me, I am sending you' (John 20:21). So this is the central question for this evening: What does it mean to be sent like Jesus?

Our Bible passage is Philippians 2:1-11, one of the high-water marks of the New Testament. We are standing on holy ground as we consider the journey of Jesus from the riches of heaven to the poverty of earth and back to the glory of heaven.

He laid aside his majesty and was born as a helpless baby; the servant King washed the dusty feet of his disciples; the suffering Saviour did not shrink from the shame of the cross; his faithful Father displayed his mighty power in raising Jesus from the dead; he was exalted to the highest place of glory; one day every knee will bow before him, and every tongue will confess Jesus Christ is Lord.

We need to remember that this gloriously rich passage was written to encourage disciples in a local church. It was written to settle disputes and tensions in a local congregation. Never be surprised at difficult relations in a local church, as living alongside other Christians can be a very dangerous thing. Working with other believers is a high-risk enterprise and we all need help if we want to harmonise. Seeing the same people every week – without getting on each other's nerves. Knowing you don't respect someone because their family life is in a shambles. Not fully trusting someone because they are not open to the Spirit, or because they are too open to the Spirit. Lacking respect for someone because they are all prayer and no action, or they are so busy in serving they never stop to meditate and pray. You can see how tensions can arise.

And we can be too sensitive and easily hurt:
'I didn't get an invitation to that special event.'
'They ignored me in church last Sunday.'
'They crossed the road when they saw me coming.'
And we hold such strong opinions about other disciples:
'They are not fit to serve as a Sunday school teacher.'
'I would never vote for that person to be a deacon.'

In one of the churches I served as pastor, a man shared with me he would not be voting for a deacon. I gently enquired why he wouldn't be voting for him. He said: 'I sat next to him at school, and he cheated in an exam.' I responded: 'That was fifty years ago.' He replied, 'But leopards don't change their spots!'

It was the school holidays and somewhere in the house a row had erupted, and the mother went to sort things out. 'What are you children quarrelling about?' she asked. The children replied: 'We are not quarrelling – we are playing pastors and deacons!'

Paul says to the church at Philippi: 'Do nothing out of selfish ambition or vain conceit. Rather, in humility value others above yourselves, not looking to your own interests but each of you to the interests of the others' (see 2:3-4).

We do tend to look to our own interests and the potential to get it wrong in relating to others. Luke's Gospel reveals a devastating weakness at the heart of the disciples. The Gospel records that on the night the Lord was betrayed; on the night he washed the feet of his disciples; on the night when he gave us the Lord's Supper, on this holy night, Luke says: 'A dispute . . . arose among them as to which of them was considered to be greatest' (Luke 22:24).

Low-life discipleship has never won the world for Christ. When we dispute who is the greatest it simply draws attention away from him who alone is *the* greatest.

Brothers and sisters, as we make a new journey with Jesus; as we dedicate ourselves afresh to win Europe for Christ; as we express our passion for freedom and justice, remember our genius is not in a great programme but in a great Saviour. We can never be sent like Jesus into this broken world while the lust for power and prestige rages in the body of Christ like a fever. The medicine which cures all our ills is this: 'Have the same [mind] as Christ' (Philippians 2:5).

So, what was in the mind of Christ when he laid aside the glory of heaven for the squalor of the stable? If we are to be sent like Jesus, what discipleship lessons do we have to learn from this Bible passage?

1. If we are sent like Jesus, there are privileges we have to relinquish

Before his birth at Bethlehem, Jesus shared the very nature of God. The Son was co-equal with the Father. He shared the supreme position of privilege in the cosmos. None of these divine attributes and powers are surrendered when Jesus is born as a baby in Bethlehem. What is surrendered is the privilege of his divine dignity. He *chose* to make himself a person of no reputation.

Adam and Eve did the opposite in the Garden of Eden. Their privileged position was Paradise, and their disposition was to grasp. They grasped and they fell. But Jesus relinquished his hold on privileges, and this is why he is heaven's champion.

This is the mind of Christ – never grasp for position and power. Always relinquish privilege for the sake of service. If you are going to be sent like Jesus, there will be privileges you will have to relinquish.

2. If we are sent like Jesus, there is a service to be rendered

What a mystery and wonder that when Jesus came from heaven as the helpless baby, he entered our world with his glory concealed.

The hands that made the stars
became the working hands in the carpenter's shop.
Jesus stands ankle-deep in wood shavings because
there was a service to be rendered.
The hands that painted the colours in the rainbow
became the helping hands around the home in Nazareth.
Jesus shared the joys and sorrows of family life
because there was a service to be rendered.
The loving hands that made us from the dust of earth
became the healing hands of Galilee.
Touching blind eyes to make them see, embracing
lepers to make them clean.
The hands that filled the oceans with water
became the serving hands in the Upper Room.

'Jesus knew that . . . he had come from God and was returning to God . . . wrapped a towel round his waist . . .' and washed the feet of his disciples' (see John 13:3-5).

If we are going to be sent like Jesus, there is a humble service we have to render.

3. If we are sent like Jesus, there is a cost to be endured

When Jesus left heaven, he stooped to conquer, but he stooped even lower in his death. His was not the death of an old man in his nineties at the end of a fruitful life of service. He did not enjoy a peaceful end in a Bethany care home surrounded by loving friends. Jesus stooped down low to the costly shame of death on the cross.

Do you remember Jesus standing on the Mount of Transfiguration? He was there with Peter, James and John and in the company of Moses and Elijah (Matthew 17:1-13). This was the moment, says F.B. Meyer, 'when his intrinsic splendour was laid aside, and it welled out in cascades and torrents of blinding light.'[24] In that moment of transfiguration, Jesus could have stepped back into the glory of heaven. But he knew he had a costly journey to make, and his footsteps had to lead him down the mountain. He had to go lower into the valley of human experience because he was called to endure death on the cross. The Bible says death on a cross was a scandal: 'anyone hung on a tree is under God's curse' (Deuteronomy 21:23, NRSVA). Popular opinion said the cross was a scandal, it was a shameful death because crucifixion did not just kill people, it tortured them to death slowly. This was the dreadful cost of the cross.

In the time when this letter of Paul was written, no one wore a cross as jewellery. No one embossed a cross on the cover of their Bible scrolls. There was no sign of a cross on the buildings where they met. Because death on the cross was shameful, slow and ignominious.

This was the cost which Jesus endured for us:

His feet walked willingly to the cross to set the captive free. His hands were nailed to the tree to break the power of sin.

---

24. F.B. Meyer, *Devotional Commentary on Philippians* (Grand Rapids, MI: Kregel Publications, 1979), p. 85.

His lifeless limbs were laid in the darkness of the tomb. So, we could walk free in the service of the King and the kingdom!

4. If we are sent like Jesus, there will be a glory to be shared

It was for the 'joy that was set before him' (Hebrews 12:2) that Jesus endured the shame and pain of the cross.

Wicked men nailed Jesus to the cross, but God displayed his mightiest power in raising Jesus from the dead and seating him at the right hand of his glory on high. What a unique God-given glory is bestowed on Jesus.

This is Jesus – who has the name above all names.
This is Jesus – the name that compels every knee to bow.
Every tongue one day will be required to confess Jesus alone is Lord.

Do you realise how radically subversive is this claim? When Paul writes this message, he is a prisoner in a cell and a powerful Roman emperor is ruling the world. The little congregation in Philippi are daily aware of the power of the Roman Empire. The city of Philippi is filled with veteran soldiers who have fought for their country, and they are passionate about patriotism. There is one king, and that is Caesar; one kingdom, and that is Rome. It is the language of treachery that suggests there is another King and kingdom.

We live today under the sway of seemingly all-powerful political and cultural empires. They demand wholehearted allegiance. We are commanded to bow the knee to a fashionable ideology or be cancelled and shamed. This is the cost to being a disciple of Jesus. We cannot offer service to another king when we have pledged allegiance to Jesus as Lord. Whatever the cost, this is our subversive story, this is our countercultural song. Every kingdom without exception will one day bow the knee to King Jesus! We are called to be what Richard John Neuhaus calls: 'premature ambassadors, having arrived at court before the sovereignty of our king has been recognised.'[25] We are designated ambassadors for Christ, and God uses our lives to make his appeal to the empires of our world. The message is simple: 'Be reconciled to God' (2 Corinthians 5:20).

If you want to be sent like Jesus,
there will be privileges to be relinquished
a humble service to be rendered
a costly discipleship to be endured
and the promise of a share in the unique glory God
has given to Jesus alone.

We are faced with a clear choice. If we want to journey with Jesus, then either we do it his way or your theme song will be that you did it your way. I have done some research on the song 'My Way' made famous by Frank Sinatra. The lyrics of the song convey the last thoughts of a dying man with the memorable strapline that he did it his way. The words of this song are the ultimate Christ-less philosophy of life. The theme verse of this Christ-less philosophy is: 'For me, to live is me alone.' Let your theme verse be: 'For me, to live is Christ and to die is gain' (Philippians 1:21).

God has shared the life of Christ with us not that we might be better behaved, but that we might be unbelievably

---

25. Richard John Neuhaus *Freedom in Ministry* (Grand Rapids, MI: Eerdmans, 1979), p. 71.

transformed into the likeness of Christ. Bearing the likeness of Christ, we are sent to be his hands and feet in this needy world.

Consider the privileges you will have to relinquish and begin to loosen your grip on power and privilege. Stop grasping at position and lay to one side your personal ambitions. Say to the Lord, 'I offer you the best and greatest in my life and freely abandon them for your loving purposes.' Think of the humble service only you can give. Can you hear the Lord saying to you today:

I need your working hands for the workplace?
I need your helping hands in the home?
I need your healing hands in all the broken places of the world?
I need your servant hands to wash the feet of those nearest to you?
I need your outstretched hands to welcome home the prodigal child?

The hardest thing is when God is not offering us a new calling, but he is asking us to make a fresh commitment to an old calling and his encouragement to us is 'keep on keeping on'.

Brothers and sisters don't avoid the cost of the cross! It is a privilege to believe in Jesus, and the greatest privilege to suffer for Christ and his gospel. The question of Jesus to his disciples comes resounding down the ages: 'Can you drink the cup I am going to drink?' (Matthew 20:22).

This was the heart of what happened in Amsterdam 400 years ago. Our mothers and fathers in the Baptist faith and tradition answered a resounding 'yes' to the question of Jesus. They did drink the costly cup of bearing the cross.

They made a bloodstained journey of discipleship that not only took them across Europe – but to all parts of the world.

The same question of Jesus rings out again – can you drink the costly cup? When the truth of the gospel offends the standards of the world, will you drink the cup of exclusion and ridicule? When loyalty to Christ brings you into conflict with the cultures of our age, will you drink the cup of disgrace and discrimination? And what of the promised glory that one day we will share with King Jesus? We have already received a downpayment of that glory which guarantees our inheritance (Ephesians 1:13-14). Jesus is King and we exalt him in our worship. The battle is over, the victory is won and the King is reigning. It is just the small matter that the world does not know it! Our mandate as ambassadors is to infiltrate the world with the message of good news:

Believe in your heart that God raised Jesus from the dead.
Confess Jesus as Lord.
Bow the knee in worship to Jesus.
Share the glory of the King.
Today is the day of opportunity!

We warn people that a tomorrow is coming when it will no longer be the day of opportunity. One day the world will wake up to discover it's too late to believe.

The doors will be shut.
The books will be opened.
There will be a dawning of terrible awareness.
So that people will be crying to the mountains and rocks,

'Fall on us and hide us from the face of him who sits on his throne'
(Revelation 6:16).

People will cry with regret: 'I never believed in my heart; I never confessed with my lips; I never bowed the knee, but I now see he is who he said he is – the Lord!' But until that awesome day comes, the doors of missionary opportunity stand open- and God is looking for a people who are willing to be sent like Jesus, men and women who will follow in the steps of Jesus. On the 3rd of May 1959 I was baptised and sang the hymn: 'O Jesus, I Have Promised'. This old hymn includes the line, 'Oh, let me see Thy footmarks, And in them plant mine own'. [26]
So let this be our prayer this evening:

Lord Jesus, I want to be sent as you were sent.
I want to make a new journey with you.
O may I see your footprints
and in them plant my own.

26. John Ernest Bode (1816-74), www.hymnal.net/en/hymn/h/465 (accessed 24.4.23).

This sermon was preached on the opening night of the Baptist World Alliance (BWA) Congress in Hawaii July 2010. The theme of the congress was 'Hear the Spirit' and I was given the Bible passage under the title 'Consecration'. The Congress in Hawaii marked the end of my five years serving as the president of the Baptist World Alliance 2005-10.

My journey had begun in Seoul, South Korea in July 2004 when I was appointed as president-elect. A year later I was inducted into the presidency at the Baptist World Congress held in Birmingham, UK.

In the five years that followed, my journeys took me to numerous locations in six of the seven continents. Regretfully, I received no invitations from Antarctica!

5

The Spirit of the Lord is Upon Me

Luke 4:18

When my friends discovered I was flying to Hawaii for the BWA Congress, they reacted in a variety of ways. Some friends were envious and said they wished they were coming with me, and others were curious and enquired why the exotic venue of Hawaii had been chosen. To which I replied, 'Why not Hawaii?' Some of my friends were full of good wishes and said they would be praying we would have a spiritually rich congress. And some added the personal comment that they considered it was romantic for my wife, Janet, and I to be in the paradise setting of Hawaii!

Now, my surname is Coffey which originates from Ireland, and I was blessed with some grandparents who were of Irish extraction. You may be aware that the Irish are renowned as incurable romantics and not surprisingly I have inherited this in my personality. A few months ago, I was at Victoria rail station in London waiting for a train. It was early morning and over the loudspeakers I heard the music of one of my wife's favourite songs so, feeling romantic, I thought I would send her a text. The text read:

'I am listening to your favourite song and thinking of you – I love you very much – David'. And then, in an act of romantic madness, I added two kisses to the text.

Now, my heart expected an instant reply from my wife but there was no response. No text. Not even a tweet, and I felt very downcast and rejected. I carried on my work through the day and completed my lectures at Spurgeon's College, and late afternoon I was on the train making my way home to Oxfordshire when I received a text. But it was not from my wife, Janet. It was from a friend of mine called Steve. His message read: 'Was this text intended for me? Are you wanting to take our relationship to a deeper level?' My message with the two kisses had gone to him! A message, intended for Janet's eyes only, had gone astray.

Now, here is the point. Every time we open God's Word there is a message for our eyes only.

As Baptists we believe that God speaks through his living Word and every day of this BWA congress there will be a personal message for us. As we come to the living Word, let us approach it as lively people expecting that God has a word for us. Don't let God's message go astray.

Our congress theme is 'Hear the Spirit' and this is unquestionably a deep challenge to all our lives and ministries. As we lead our churches and manage our Christian organisations, the question is, which spirit is guiding our thinking? Is it the self-dependent spirit that imagines the harder you work, the more you achieve? A worldly spirit of activism can invade the life of the Church and lead us to believe that as long as we are busy with our programmes and strategies, we are guaranteed spiritual blessing.

Specific strategies and managed programmes do have the potential to enrich our mission and bless a needy world, but I urge you to heed this warning about the true source of our spiritual energy and vision. You can be a purpose-driven church; a seeker-sensitive church; an emergent and creative church; a justice and peace church; a Reformed Calvinist church. But whatever the tradition of our church, if we fail to hear the Holy Spirit of the Living God, then all our serving will be futile and fruitless.

I urge you to never embark on your ministry without listening to the Spirit. It is possible to have the appointing without the anointing. You can have all the appointments but none of the anointments; you can have all the titles but none of the authority; you can have all the programmes but none of the power of the Spirit. Seek the anointing of the Holy Spirit on your life and ministry! This was the way of Jesus. He was the one who commenced his mission ministry in the pulpit at Nazareth with the words 'The Spirit of the Lord is on me because he has anointed me . . .' (Luke 4:18).

Luke clearly states that through the whole of his life, Jesus operated in the realm of the Spirit. The Holy Spirit was integral to his virgin birth because Jesus was conceived by the Holy Spirit and born of the virgin Mary (Luke 1:34-35). At his baptism the divine identity of Jesus was affirmed by an action of the Holy Spirit. The heaven was opened, and the Holy Spirit descended upon Jesus 'in bodily form like a dove', and the voice came from heaven: 'You are my Son, whom I love; with you I am well pleased' (Luke 3:21-22).

Then, full of the Holy Spirit, Jesus was led by the Spirit into the wilderness of temptation where for forty days he was tempted by the devil (Luke 4:1-13). This is the testing of Jesus' consecration to God. Will he serve God's way and will and trust God to provide for his needs? Jesus battles with the web of lies that will lead him away from the path of servant leadership.

In the power of the Spirit, Jesus defeats Satan and emerges victorious from the wilderness of temptations.

It's as if Jesus draws a line in the sand of the desert and proclaims: 'I will serve God's way or not at all.' Then, following these desert temptations, Jesus is filled with the Holy Spirit and commences his teaching and healing ministry. He stands in the Nazareth pulpit and proclaims boldly: 'The Spirit of the Lord is on me' (Luke 4:18).

Friends, can you see from the plain teaching of the Gospel record that the Spirit of the Lord is upon Jesus for his earthly origins, his messianic identity and his power to preach and heal? So why is it that so often in our ministries we choose to go it alone? This congress theme of 'Hear the Spirit' could be a most significant moment in the history of our movement because so often as Baptists we are deaf to the Spirit. We choose *our* way, *our* methods and *our* timing.

When we behave like this, I suggest we are not walking in the footsteps of those Baptists who have gone before. John Smyth and Thomas Helwys heard the Spirit as our fledging movement was founded in Amsterdam in 1609. It was because Lottie Moon[27] and Martin Luther King heard the Spirit in their lifetime that they accomplished great things for Jesus Christ. If these men and women had been deaf to the Spirit then, God would never have recorded their names in his book of spiritual heroes.

God's purpose is that the Spirit-filled ministry of Jesus should continue today through all his people. Jesus promised the gift of his Holy Spirit in his farewell words: 'You will have power to be my witnesses when the Holy Spirit comes' (see Acts 1:8). On the day of Pentecost, Jesus fulfilled his promise and sent us the gift of his Spirit, and now the Lord of the Church expects all his people to say:

---

27. Missionary to China.

The Spirit of the Lord is upon me, I am an anointed person.

The essence of the Holy Spirit's ministry is to bring the presence of Christ to his people.

God's purpose is that the Lord Jesus Christ is loved, honoured and praised (John 16:14). The desire of the Holy Spirit is to see Jesus pre-eminent in his Church.

Jim Packer suggests:

> It is as if the Spirit stands behind us, throwing light over our shoulder, on Jesus, who stands facing us. The message of the Holy Spirit is never: 'Look at me; listen to me; come to me; get to know me,' but always, 'Look at *him*, and see his glory; listen to *him*, and hear his word; go to *him*, and have life; get to know *him*, and taste his gift of joy and peace.'[28]

We have arrived in the beautiful land of Hawaii ready to enjoy some new experiences this week. We have already encountered the unique *Aloha* spirit of Hawaii – truly the warmth and hospitality of Hawaiian people is a wonderful experience.

With invitations to the Polynesian Cultural Centre and the historic Pearl Harbour we are guaranteed many new experiences this congress week. But there are two key spiritual experiences you need to be sure about if you want God's best from this congress.

You need to testify first that the Holy Spirit is in me, and second that the Holy Spirit is on me. For if you cannot say

---

28. J.I. Packer *Keep In Step with the Spirit: Finding Fullness in Our Walk With God* (Nottingham: IVP, 2005), p.57.

'the Holy Spirit is in me', then you cannot be truly part of God's family. If you are unable to say 'the Holy Spirit is on me', then you will never be effective in your ministry.

If you say to me this evening: 'David, how can I experience these truths personally?' Then my answer would be to ask if you have been born again of the Spirit by faith in Jesus? Have you received by God's grace the gift of new life? Are you able to say: 'I have been crucified with Christ and I no longer live, but Christ lives in me. The life I now live . . . I live by faith in the Son of God, who loved me and [died] for me' (Galatians 2:20)?

When the Holy Spirit is in you, then the love of God is poured into your heart (Romans 5:5). Some of you can testify this evening to the inner courage the Holy Spirit gives us. When you were standing in a courtroom on trial for being a follower of Jesus, the Holy Spirit made you a bold witness and taught you 'at the very hour' what to say (Luke 12:12, ESV). Many of you here have experienced the comforting peace of the Holy Spirit during the great storms of life (John 14:16).

We have stood in solidarity this year with those who suffered because of the devastating storms of sorrow and destruction which suddenly came upon the nations of Haiti and Chile. When your little ship has been tossed about on the great oceans of life, and you limp into a safe harbour with your broken mast and torn sails and missing rudder, what testimony have you been able to declare to a watching world? Those who know the inner peace of the Holy Spirit, the Comforter, are the ones who can testify: 'When I passed through the waters I did not drown' (see Isaiah 43:2) and 'At the height of the storm, Jesus was with me'.

But if we know the Holy Spirit is in us, how can we be sure the Holy Spirit is on us? When the Holy Spirit is on us, it shows because those who hear the Spirit follow the directions of Jesus. They are serious about obeying his words. This was the pattern of Jesus' life. He declared he could do nothing by himself. He could only do what he saw the Father doing (John 5:19). Jesus as the Son of God imitated his heavenly Father.

I am not sure a father and his son understood this spiritual principle of imitation. The father was going away from home on a business trip and said to his nine-year-old son that he wanted him to help around the house while he was away. The father said to the boy: 'I want you to do what I normally do.' The father had in mind clearing the dinner table; washing the dishes; putting out the rubbish bins. After a few days the father returned from his business trip and asked his wife: 'How did our son do while I was away?' His wife replied: 'It was very strange. After breakfast, our son made himself a cup of coffee and went into the living room and sat down. He put on some loud music and read the newspaper for half an hour.'

Be sure what you are modelling in your life is an example worth imitating!

Jesus said, 'The Son can do nothing by himself; he can do only what he sees his Father doing, because whatever the Father does the Son also does' (John 5:19). This is the pattern of life in the Spirit. When we listen to the Holy Spirit we can live in perfect harmony with the Holy Trinity. To paraphrase the words of Jesus: 'You cannot do anything by yourselves; you can only do what you see me doing.'

When the Holy Spirit is on us, and Jesus is leading his people, it shows. The Acts of the Apostles is an inspiring account of what happens when people listen to the Spirit and follow Jesus on mission. In page after page of Acts we see that when the Holy Spirit is on people it produces healthy churches and fruitful mission; the Holy Spirit inspires praise and worship; he creates fellowship between diverse people; he gives wisdom and discernment; he exposes dishonesty in the Church; he guides people in choosing church leaders; he drives the Church into the adventures of evangelism; he brings us to new mission frontiers and encourages us to cross boundaries.

But the greatest sign that the Holy Spirit is on us is when we discover that God has included us in his action plan for winning a lost world. It's a *kairos* moment when we realise our calling is not to be passive spectators, but called and gifted actors in the unfolding drama of salvation's story.

You are probably aware that Honolulu is a major centre for the film industry. Twenty minutes' drive from this Congress Hall is the film set for the cult TV series *Lost*. In June 2010, Walt Disney productions began making *On Stranger Tides*, the latest movie in the *Pirates of the Caribbean* series. The long-running television series *Hawaii Five-O* was filmed in this city and the 2010 remake series will soon be released.

Now, I confess I enjoy the occasional visit to the movies and have sat in a darkened theatre with my popcorn and coke. This is fine for when we are relaxing, but it is an unsuitable culture for mission ministry because the Holy Spirit is not interested in a spectator culture. We are not meant to sit back as if in a darkened movie theatre, watching a needy world flicker before our eyes.

God does not intend us to be passive spectators, he has called and equipped us to be the actors in his great drama and has a part for each of us in his unfolding story of salvation. There is no application form to fill in; there is no audition to attend; all it requires is for every child of God to wake up and realise that the Spirit of the Lord is on them and he has anointed us for service in his world. This gift is not just for preachers and pastors and missionaries, it is a promise for all followers of Jesus Christ.

When the Holy Spirit is upon us, the anointing shows. And this anointing enables us to face the most challenging of tasks.

Jesus chose Isaiah 61 as the starting point for his sermon in Nazareth where Isaiah describes scenes of utter devastation. There are ruined buildings and desolate communities; rundown cities filled with broken-hearted people wearing sackcloth and ashes; places of devastation where people feel they are trapped in a prison of hopelessness; people are burdened by poverty and spiritual blindness and crying out for a new beginning.

Isaiah faced an inherited brokenness with communities that had been devastated for generations (Isaiah 61:4). Do you realise the implications of this inherited brokenness? It means you could be facing a roadblock in your ministry caused by a previous generation. The cause of the roadblock happened long before you arrived on the scene, but the impact of the inherited brokenness means people feel they are ruined forever. Their disposition is that nothing can change their situation because there has been devastation for generations, and this creates a climate of extreme hopelessness.

Jesus faced this on the day he came to Nazareth. He looked out on a congregation which represented the inherited brokenness of the villages and cities of his day. The families of poor farmers who were burdened because of harsh taxation systems (Luke 19:8); people whose lives had been destroyed by shame and guilt (Luke 7:36-50); the helplessness of people who had spent all their money on doctors and still were not cured (Luke 8:43); a community attempting to cope with the man who was called a hopeless case. People did not know how to cope with his demon possession, so they wrapped him in chains and kept him under guard in the town cemetery (Luke 8:26-39). This is a portrait of the despair of inherited brokenness.

Jesus faced a broken world of inherited brokenness. Here we are in paradise for a few days, but soon we will return home where, daily, we face the corrosive blight of inherited brokenness.

We have left behind scenes of utter devastation with ruined buildings and desolate communities. Many of us work in rundown cities filled with broken-hearted people. We minister to people who feel they are trapped in prisons of hopelessness and perhaps we have come to this congress crying to the Lord for a new beginning for our mission ministry.

Your heart cry is to ask the Lord to give you a breakthrough with this inherited brokenness.

You know it has held back your church or organisation through generations of devastation.

Well, I have good news for you. When the person anointed with the Holy Spirit speaks, then the lives of people are transformed. The broken-hearted are healed; the bound are delivered; the prisoners are released (Isaiah 61:1). When the Spirit of the Lord is on us, even bricks and mortar can be changed.

The unfolding of the year of the Lord's favour means that ancient ruins are rebuilt; waste places are restored; ruined cities are renewed (Isaiah 61:4). The joyful message of Jubilee rolls back the years of devastation.

Surely all of us want to see the healing of this inherited brokenness in our communities? We are the followers of Jesus Christ who believe his Church is called and created to make a difference in his world. We are the sent ones who have the words of Jesus burned into our lives: 'As the Father has sent me, I am sending you' (John 20:21).

We know that Jesus breathed on his disciples and said 'Receive the Holy Spirit' (John 20:22) and therefore our prayer this evening should be: 'Lord Jesus, breathe on us, for when we have the anointing of the Spirit, our world can be changed.'

Jesus said he shared his authority with his disciples (Luke 10:19) so why is it we stumble around the world as if we are a little people? We behave as if we are nobodies, but God says we are a chosen people. We say we have no status, but God says we are a royal priesthood. We declare we are unimportant, but God has granted us the title of 'a holy nation' (1 Peter 2:9). Surely when the Spirit of the Lord is on us, we should be deeply aware that we are the children of the King! These privileges indicate we are never a little people in God's eyes.

Many years ago in Birmingham, England, there was a large department store and adjacent to the store was a Friends meeting house. Just a small building where the Quakers worshipped. One day the owners of the store wrote a letter to the Quakers sharing they had plans to expand their business and needed more land to build bigger premises. The letter concluded by asking the members to name the price of the building as they wanted to purchase it. The Quaker leadership read the letter and after a few days they sent their reply. They said they were grateful the large store had shared their plans for growth and expansion. But as it happened, The Quakers were also thinking of expanding and would like to grow and develop on the same site. They invited the owners to name their price and offered to buy their store!

The members of the Friends meeting house were not fooling with the owners of the department store because they had the resources to buy the store. The signature at the foot of the letter said it all. The letter had been signed by John Cadbury, who was the wealthy chocolate manufacturer and also a committed Quaker Christian. With his wealth he could have probably purchased every department store in the country![29]

Brothers and sisters, the people of God are never a little people. The world may despise and hate us; the world may persecute us and seek to destroy us; the world may exercise a might without morality and a power without compassion. But the truth is when the world has left the battlefield, the last people standing will be those who will exclaim: 'The Spirit of the Lord is upon us because he has anointed us.'

God can give you a fresh anointing of his Holy Spirit this evening to enable you to speak with power and serve with authority. You can experience the appointing and the anointing. You can enjoy the programme and the power. You can carry all your privileged titles with spiritual authority. The Lord desires you to finish the work he has given you to do.

Jesus says to us this evening:

Finish the ministry I have given you to do.
Does not all I have done for you inspire you to do your best for me?
And our response must be to offer a prayer of consecration at the beginning of this congress:

---

29. Dr Donald English CBE (1930-98) shared this story with me. He served as moderator of the Free Churches and was elected twice as the president of the Methodist Conference.

Breathe on me, Breath of God:
fill me with life anew,
that I may love what Thou dost love
and do what Thou wouldst do.[30]

---

30. Edwin Hatch (1835-89), 'Breathe on Me, Breath of God', www.christianwebresources. co.uk/hymns/hymn/62/ (accessed 24.4.23).

I preached this sermon at Totnes United Free Church, Devon, on the first Sunday of Advent in 2021. I had the privilege of mentoring their gifted pastor, Ade Gascoyne, for three years after his ordination.

Whenever I have led a pilgrimage to the Holy Land, one of the highlights is to visit modern day Bethlehem and stand in the fields outside and read the book of Ruth.

The Christian presence in Bethlehem is in rapid decline and we need the core message of this book to remind us that, however chaotic and dangerous the world may become, God is always working out his loving purposes.

Give God time.

6

Recovering From the Big Mistakes of Life

Ruth 1

The popular BBC programme, *Who Do You Think You Are?*, reminds us that exploring a family tree can be full of surprises. This is true when you explore the details of the family tree of Jesus in Matthew 1.

There is a lying husband who pretends his wife is his sister; the head of the royal family who commits adultery and arranges for the husband of the woman he has slept with to be bumped off; then there is the immigrant woman called Ruth who comes from a pagan background and marries into a family that believes in God.

Ruth is so important a relative of Jesus that she has a whole book of the Old Testament devoted to her life story. One of the traditions of the Advent season for Christians is to read the Old Testament stories that point to the coming of Jesus. It's a great way to prepare for Christmas.

Let's remind ourselves of this story from the book of Ruth which took place just over 1,000 years before Jesus was born in Bethlehem. The book opens with the words:

'In the days when the judges ruled, there was a famine in the land' (1:1).

In the days when the judges ruled Israel there was *political chaos*. Read the last verse of the previous book which sums up the spirit of the age: 'In those days Israel had no king – everyone did [what was right in their eyes]' (Judges 21:25). So we discover that 3,000 years ago there was a 'me first' generation.

There was also *moral decay* in the nation. The gruesome narrative in Judges 19 offers a glimpse into the decadent life of the nation. It is a familiar story of binge drinking and gang rape and the death of a young woman. Her husband was so distraught that he cut her dead body into twelve pieces and sent them to all parts of the nation. A shocked population responded: 'We have never seen anything like this in our lifetime' (see Judges 19:30).

There was *economic hardship* provoked by a famine in the land. Remember, our Bible story centres on Bethlehem, whose name means 'house of bread'. Bethlehem was the grain store for the region, a distribution hub for bread supplies. If there was famine in the house of bread, then it is a truly critical moment for the nation.

With just a few words, the writer has described the crisis for those living in Bethlehem. There was political chaos, moral decay and economic hardship. But like any gripping documentary, the writer focuses on one family. How was life for an average family in Bethlehem?

We are now introduced to a man called Elimelek, his wife, Naomi, and their two sons, Mahlon and Kilion. With all the chaos and uncertainty, they decide to pack up and leave Bethlehem and move to a place called Moab. This decision may appear as basic as someone deciding to move home from Totnes to Tunbridge Wells. But dig deeper into their names and you realise the writer may be telling us the move of this family was an error of judgement. The biggest mistake they could make.

The father's name was Elimelek which means 'My God is king'. This indicates Elimelek's family had a rich heritage of trusting God. They were believers and Elimelek should have known from his spiritual background that when times are tough you don't walk away, you stay where you are and trust God to perform his miracles in difficult places.

But the family chose not to trust God to provide for them and set off on their self-made adventure. Of all the places the family chose to make their home, they landed in the country of Moab. This nation was the mecca for dark pagan religion. The Moabites sacrificed children to appease the god they worshipped. Moabites had been the fierce enemies of Israel for eighteen years. It was the last place on earth you would expect to find a faithful believer in God moving to.

Within a short period of time of moving from Bethlehem to Moab, tragedy strikes when Elimelek dies and his wife, Naomi, is left a widow with two sons. The sons marry local girls, Orpah and Ruth, reared in the Moabite culture. After ten years, both of Naomi's sons die and you now have three widows living under one roof. It's a house of deep sadness. With wonderful skill the writer turns their attention to the relationship between mother-in-law Naomi and her two daughters-in-law.

Luis Palau was a world-famous evangelist. Born in Argentina, he moved in his mid-twenties and made his home Portland, Oregon, USA. He was a gifted communicator of the gospel and a few years ago I was sharing a conference with him at the Keswick Convention. Knowing his use of humour, I asked him what story went down well in every country of the world. Without hesitating he said mother-in-law jokes! He said: 'I have visited over seventy nations and I only have to say, "I'm having problems with my mother-in-law" and the place erupts in laughter.'

I'm not making any mother-in-law jokes this morning! Instead, I want to present to you this stunning mother-in-law called Naomi. It's worth pausing to observe what makes her a wonderful mother-in-law. First, we know she was *a caring woman.* She had kept in touch with her family back home in Bethlehem and it can't have been a blessing to the bereaved Naomi to hear the news that life had returned to normal in Bethlehem. God had 'come to the aid of his people by providing food for them' (v. 6). The little town was once again the house of bread. If I was Naomi, I would certainly ask the question: Why on earth did we leave Bethlehem?

Naomi makes the decision to travel back home to her much-loved Bethlehem and further reveals her caring nature when she suggests to her daughters-in-law she didn't expect them to make the journey. 'Go back and live with your mothers and I will make my way home' (see v. 8).

She was also *a spiritual woman* and from a broken heart was able to bless her daughters-in-law. 'May God be kind to you just as you've been kind to me and my dead sons. I hope will you both find husbands' (see vv. 8-9).

Naomi was caring, spiritual and *she was humorous.* When the two girls begin weeping and express the desire to stay with Naomi and join her for the journey back to Bethlehem, Naomi says: 'Are you girls expecting me to produce two more sons for you to marry? I'm too old to marry again, but if I did find a man to marry me tonight, and I conceived immediately, are you prepared to wait for years until these two boys grow up?' (v. 11). Naomi might have added: 'And what happens, having waited for the boys to come to maturity that you don't like either of them!'

But note the fourth aspect of her personality – Naomi was *transparently honest*. She has reflected on everything that has happened to her over the past few years, including the big mistake of the house move, and has come to the conclusion that the Lord's hand has turned against her. She is convinced that God doesn't like her, and he has made her life 'very bitter' (v. 20).

It's a sobering experience to witness the raw anger of a believer who thinks the Almighty has made their life bitter. When people are passing through a bitter experience, they often turn their anger on people. I can recall a church meeting where a normally calm and peaceful Christian woman let rip with a volley of grievances against me as the pastor as well as the church fellowship. I visited the woman and her husband and listened to their story. Their experience was very similar to Naomi, and they felt that God had turned his back on their family life.

If you journey with the psalmist, you will discover words which express a deep disappointment with God. 'Is he deaf? Why doesn't he hear me? Why am I in this mess?' Wicked people appear to be prospering while good people continue to suffer. *The Message* version expresses memorably this verse:

Don't turn a deaf ear when I call you, GOD.
If all I get from you is deafening silence,
I'd be better off in the Black Hole.
(Psalm 28:1)

Naomi is not unusual for feeling bitter towards God and for saying publicly that she feels the Lord's hand has gone against her. It happens. Our danger, when we are bitter with God, is we think we are a rubbish believer and God can never use us.

But look at this marvellous moment in the story in verses 14-18. Naomi has decided to return to Bethlehem, but her daughter-in-law Oprah opts to stay in Moab, and kisses Naomi farewell. Despite Naomi suggesting to Ruth that she does the same, she clings to Naomi, and we then read one of the most lyrically moving speeches in all the Bible.

Ruth has lost her husband and she knows what it is to grieve. She understands why Naomi's heart has been broken in pieces, three times. Ruth has heard Naomi pour out her bitter disappointment with the Almighty. Now this is Ruth's awesome response to what she has seen in Naomi's broken and bitter life:

Don't urge me to leave you or to turn back from you.
Where you go, I will go, and where you stay, I will stay.
Your people will be my people, and your God my God.
Where you die I will die, and there I will be buried.
May the LORD deal with me, be it ever so severely, if even death separates you and me.
(vv. 16-17)

I want each Naomi this morning to hear this word of encouragement. Even when you think you are a rubbish believer because you are bitter towards the Almighty, God can use your broken life. Ruth has glimpsed something spiritually real in the rawness of Naomi's bitter grief and disillusion with God. How else can Ruth make the statement: 'I want your people to be my people and your God to be my God'?

The two widows return to Bethlehem and when they arrive, old friends are startled by the appearance of Naomi. They even question whether this is the same woman who used to be their neighbour. The years of sadness, grief and anxiety had not been kind to Naomi. Her physical appearance had altered. Naomi must have read their thoughts as she explains she has changed her name. 'I know my name Naomi means pleasant, but I'm changing my name to Mara which means bitter woman. Please call me Mara, because God has marred my life. I'm bitter because the Almighty has made my life very bitter. I went away full and the Lord has brought me back empty. The Lord has afflicted me, and the Almighty has brought me misfortune. So please don't call me Naomi' (based on vv. 20-21).

What is interesting is the Hebrew name Naomi uses for God is not the normal title a sincere believer would use. Normally the word is Yahweh, which is the close personal covenant name. Instead she uses the Hebrew name for Almighty which is El Shaddai.

Naomi says El Shaddai has brought her misfortune. This word conveys rock-like strength and stability. The Almighty one is able to triumph over every obstacle. Naomi is saying to El Shaddai: 'I am not holding anything back from you because I believe you are strong enough to take my pain and bitterness.'

Naomi takes the heavy burden of her pain and bitterness and lays it before the Lord, who she believes is strong enough to bear her burdens:

The bitter experience of her triple bereavement.
The sudden loss of her husband and two sons.
The mystery of why all this has happened to her.

The question as to why they left Bethlehem.
She declares her deep disappointment with God.
She doesn't deny the conviction of her heart –
that the Lord has brought misfortune and sadness into
her life.
She lays this heavy burden at the feet of El Shaddai –
the Almighty One.

Naomi and Ruth are always somewhere in a congregation. Naomi is hanging on by her spiritual fingernails. This caring, spiritual, humorous, transparently honest woman is casting all her burdens on El Shaddai.

Ruth is also a special woman who has none of the advantages of a long spiritual heritage in the living God. But she has seen enough in the life of her mother-in-law to make her spiritually curious. She observes a quality of genuine faith she finds very attractive. Ruth has been living off Naomi's faith, but the time has now come for her to have a faith of her own, which is why she testifies to Naomi: 'I want your God to be my God.'

I invite Naomi to come to the cross of Jesus with all the pain and bitter sadness of your life. Open your heart to El Shaddai and allow the Almighty One to provide you with his peace and comfort and the promise of a new beginning. And Ruth, you are invited to come to the same cross of Jesus Christ and receive your own personal gift of faith in Jesus. A faith you can call your own.

If you visit the chapel of Spurgeon's College, as you enter you will see a large gold-coloured cross at the front of the chapel. Floodlit from both sides it is a striking dominant image which captures the eye immediately. But if you walk slowly to the cross and stand very close you realise it is an embroidered cross and embedded in the intricate embroidery are the words of Isaiah chapter 53.

Verse 5 says:

He was pierced for our transgressions, he was crushed for our iniquities;
the punishment that brought us peace was on him, and by his wounds we are healed.

It is only by drawing near to the cross that you understand how much Jesus loves you, and you discover how much he has done to ransom, heal and restore your life.

I suggest you go home and read the remaining chapters in the book of Ruth. It will take you twenty minutes to discover how the lives of Ruth and Naomi were transformed by meeting a wealthy man called Boaz who marries Ruth. They have a son called Obed, and he was the father of Jesse whose son was none other than King David, the greatest of the Old Testament kings.

King David and his descendants feature in the family tree of Jesus in Matthew 1.

And remember what the angels said to the shepherds on the hills outside Bethlehem: 'Today in the town of David a Saviour has been born . . . Christ the Lord' (Luke 2:11, NIV 1984).

The book of Ruth is a reminder of that great promise in the New Testament, that God is able 'to do far more abundantly' (ESV) than we can 'ask or imagine' (Ephesians 3:20). He can take the big mistakes of our life and transform them by his compassion and power. Trust him today with all your heart and then, like Ruth and Naomi, watch to see the fingerprints of God weaving their way into your own life story.

I entered Spurgeon's College London in 1963, and the following four years of ministerial formation shaped my pastoral and preaching ministry for the decades that followed.

This is the sermon I preached at Spurgeon's Graduation and Commissioning Service held at the Fairfield Halls, Croydon on the 24 June 2006. It was the 150th anniversary year of the college founded by Charles Haddon Spurgeon.

In 1854, aged just nineteen, Spurgeon was called to the pastorate of the famed New Park Street Chapel London, and after seven years the congregation moved to the purpose-built Metropolitan Tabernacle at the Elephant and Castle, London.

The new church seated 5,000 people with further room for 1,000 standing. He pastored this London congregation for thirty-eight years before his death in 1892 aged fifty-seven.

Spurgeon's advice to his students was to be determined to preach the gospel plainly and simply so that everybody may understand it.

7

Don't Lose Heart!

2 Corinthians 4

It was thirty-nine years ago this month that I was commissioned into Christian ministry from Spurgeon's College, and my text on that day was Paul's words from Acts 20:24: 'However, I consider my life worth nothing to me, if only I may finish the race and complete the task the Lord Jesus has given me – the task of testifying to the gospel of God's grace' (NIV 1984).

I don't know what motivated my choice of the text, but reading it now, I realise it was an inspired choice. With its emphasis on finishing the race and completing the task it says one of the most important things concerning Christian ministry. Anyone can start a race but finishing the race and completing the task are what matters.

This is a great day in your lives as graduates of Spurgeon's. The exams are over, and the essays are done. The dissertations are completed and most of you know where you will be exercising your ministry. If you ask me for advice for those entering Christian ministry, I will say in the words of this passage: 'Don't lose heart.'

Twice Paul uses this phrase in 2 Corinthians 4 verses 1 and 16, because:

You can lose heart in ministry.
You can lose heart as a church.
You can lose heart as a follower of Jesus.
You can lose heart when you cannot see where God is working his world.

So, what is the antidote for not losing heart?

1. Don't lose heart over your calling (4:1)

I recall reading the story of a young minister who, ten years into his ministry, hit a crisis point over his call. He had been born into a loving Christian family where his parents had nurtured a call on his life from an early age. During his personal crisis he recorded: 'I am never sure whether I am in ministry because I have been called by God, or sent by my mother.'[31]
Let there be no confusion! God is in charge of the events of your life. You are called of God. You did not dream this up and it was not your best idea. You are called by God's mercy.
God's mercy was Paul's great theme. It was like a golden thread running through his life. He knew that all he was achieving in his ministry was by God's mercy. He saw this in the way the church began in the city of Philippi with a group of praying women led by a woman called Lydia. As Paul shared the message of the gospel, the Lord opened Lydia's

31. Source unknown.

heart to respond to his message (Acts 16:14). He confirms this initiative of God when later he writes his letter to the church: '[God] who began a good work in you will bring it to completion' (Philippians 1:6, ESV). The Lord is saying to the young church: 'I have started, so I will finish!'

It is essential to remember we don't choose Jesus – he chooses us. It is by God's mercy we are engaged in this ministry. It is the prime reason we do not lose heart.

God in his mercy has called you and therefore in your faithful discipleship you *are* going to finish the race and complete the task. When you have nothing else to cling to, simply hold on to the call given by God's great mercy.

2. Don't lose heart over your message (4:2)

Two thousand years ago, the city of Corinth was a challenging location to be a believer. It was a mad, bad and dangerous city in which to follow Jesus. Paul summarises the challenge of preaching the story of the crucified Christ in Corinth as 'a stumbling-block to Jews and foolishness to Gentiles' (1 Corinthians 1:23). Never imagine it was easier to be a believer in the first century than it is today. As Michael Green observes, the early Christians had a bad press:

To the Greeks, the message of these Christians was mad. To the Romans it was weak, and to the Jews it was incredible. Everywhere Christians were opposed as anti-social, atheistic and depraved. They had a very bad press.[32]

---

32. Michael Green, *30 Years That Changed the World: A Fresh Look at the Book of Acts* (IVP: Nottingham, 2002), p. 17.

To counter the loss of heart in the congregation, there would be great emphasis on absorbing the teaching of Jesus especially from the Sermon on the Mount with his watchword: don't be like them – be different (Matthew 6:8).

Every generation of Christians has been tempted to question whether the gospel message is big enough to face the challenges of the world. The antidote to losing heart in the message is to renounce secret, shameful and cunning methods of preaching. Never use deception and refuse to distort the Word of God. Aim to be open, truthful and honest in a 'me first' culture (v. 2).

> We preach the cross:
> You die to self in order to live for Christ.
> We preach that discipleship is costly:
> You take up your cross daily and follow Jesus
> We preach the freedoms of the gospel:
> Rules and regulations are not the lifeblood of the Church.

Honest and open preachers find their power not in sermons but in the message of their sermons. It's not the talents of a gifted preacher but the power of a preached gospel.

Don't water down the message and you will never lose heart.

3. Don't lose heart over your friends and family (4:3-6)

It is a disheartening experience in ministry when your friends and family don't make sense of the story of Jesus. People do not always understand the gospel the first time they hear it explained to them and we can lose heart in ministry because of it. We pour out our hearts in sharing our faith and people remain in the dark.

They will comment, 'The light hasn't dawned' or 'I am 90 per cent there'. They can't make sense of the story of Jesus and the spiritual reason is blindness. They self-diagnose their spiritual condition with the words 'I don't see'.

The cause and cure of this spiritual blindness are outlined in these verses:

> The god of this age has blinded the minds of the unbelievers, to keep them from seeing the light of the gospel of the glory of Christ, who is the image of God ... but God has shone his light in our hearts ...
>
> *(based on vv.4-6)*

The enemy attempts to blind the unbeliever, but it is the Holy Spirit who opens the eyes of people to see the gospel of Christ. Tom Wright says when God works through the preaching of the gospel, through the work of the Spirit: 'People come to understand all these things about themselves, about the world, about God and about Jesus. And supremely they come to the knowledge of the glory of God.'[33]

It is likened to the morning of creation when God said: 'Let there be light' (Genesis 1:3). Just as the light shone in the darkness, so God is able to make his light shine in human hearts (v. 6).

When you are tempted to lose heart over friends who suffer with spiritual blindness:

---

33. Tom Wright, *Reflecting the Glory* (Abingdon: Bible Reading Fellowship, 1997), p. 32.

Walk more closely in their shoes.

Listen more carefully to their questions.

Pray more fervently that God will perform his eye-opening ministry.

Many years ago, I preached at a baptismal service and heard an old man give his testimony. His daughter had become a Christian and she faithfully prayed for her dad that he would have his eyes opened to received Jesus as his Saviour and Lord. On the night of his baptism, the old man was asked by the pastor what the influences were that helped him come to a living faith. I suspect the pastor was hoping the man would say: 'It was one of your marvellous sermons'! Instead, the old man quietly said: 'I saw Jesus in my daughter.'

4. Don't lost heart over your circumstances (4:7-12)

On this Graduation and Commissioning Day, you are a very special group of people.

Today you are the award winners, the Spurgeon's class of 2006. What a splendid display of gifted and talented people. But let me bring you down to earth with a sober reminder.

All of us here today are very ordinary people. We are described as 'jars of clay' in which God places the treasure of his gospel (v. 7).

The treasure of the gospel is rooted in the clay jar of our vulnerable lives. That strange mixture we are as human beings.

We are fragile and can crack and go to pieces.
We easily lose heart over our circumstances.
We feel crushing anxiety, sadness and grief.
We can crumble emotionally and be filled with despair.

I like Tom Wright's translation of verse 7: 'We are battered old flowerpots filled with the glory of God.'[34] Paul provides a vivid description of just how vulnerable we are as 'battered flowerpots'. He explains why God has made us like this. It is in order that we know the power for living the Christian life is not from us but God. 'The all-surpassing [extraordinary] power is from God [not ourselves]' (v. 7). He has these memorable cutting-edge phrases describing our vulnerability. 'We are hard pressed . . . perplexed . . . persecuted . . . [physically and emotionally beaten]' (see vv. 8-9) and this language is an accurate description of the experience for all of us:

There are times when we are hard pressed –
Feeling as though life is being crushed out of us.
There are times when we are perplexed –
Feeling deeply depressed at the possible outcomes.
There are times when we feel 'persecuted' –
Feeling utterly forsaken, abandoned and lonely.
There are times when we are physically and emotionally beaten –
Wondering whether we will survive another week in ministry.

We know these feelings and they drain the life out of us. We can lose heart because of our vulnerability. But listen

---

34. Ibid., p. 34.

carefully to what these verses are saying. Because the indestructible treasure of the risen life of Jesus is imbedded in your vulnerable life, you can interpret your story through his story: 'We always carry around in our body the death of Jesus, so that the life of Jesus may also be revealed in our body' (v. 10.)

When I feel I am being led like an innocent lamb,
And I am too weak to carry the cross I know is mine,
And I am lying helpless in a coffin of deadly despair,
In that moment I can hear the resurrection command
of the risen Lord:
'Live again!'
He can breathe new life into my spirit.
Dying and rising with Jesus is *the* antidote to our
vulnerability.
You will be hard pressed, and it will feel like a dying
moment.
But the resurrection life within you means you will
never be crushed.
You will be perplexed – but never to the point of despair.
You may be persecuted – but you will never be
abandoned by God.
You may be struck down – but you will not be destroyed.
Because your life is 'hidden with Christ in God'
(Colossians 3:3).
Just because you are vulnerable, is no reason to lose
heart.
This is the way God chooses to make his strength
perfect in our weakness (see 2 Corinthians 12:9).

5. Don't lose heart over your future (4:16-17).

These verses are an astonishing statement on the ageing process. We are not to lose heart because even though we are outwardly 'wasting away', inwardly we are being daily renewed.

Paul calculates that all the sorrows, difficulties and disappointments of life, including the 'wasting away' of the ageing process, should be considered as slight, momentary and temporary compared to the Holy Spirit's work of inward renewal (vv. 17-18). In verse 17 he compares a contrast of weights. The lightweight burden of suffering on earth with the heavyweight future glory outweighs our present burdens. God has put a piece of new heaven and new earth in our hearts which is downpayment of glory with much more to come!

My beloved mother died last month aged ninety-three. She was a wonderful Christian with a host of friends, and without doubt my best prayer warrior. Family and friends attended an inspiring service of thanksgiving for her life and ministry. In her later years, friends who had known her through many years of active Christian service would say to me: 'Your poor mother is a shadow of the person she used to be.' I had to respond by saying: 'You are wrong – my mother is a shadow of the person she is *going* to be.'

This is the final reason for the 'Don't lose heart' sayings of this chapter. 'Outwardly we are wasting away' but 'inwardly we are being renewed'. Everything we can see with the human eye is temporary and is outwardly wasting away. You will lose heart if your sole focus is on what you can manage and organise. Remember, that which you can manage and organise is temporary. Instead, focus on things you can't organise and the things you can't see. This is the thrust of the Scripture passage. We are being invited to develop a way of seeing with the eye of faith. Look back with the eye of faith to the cross and resurrection of Jesus. Look around with the eye of faith and see what God is doing today. Look ahead with the eye of faith and see what God has prepared for his people.

Never be pushed along by a raw activism that seeks to bring in the kingdom of God. Instead, be lured by the heavenly vision of a renewed creation, a redeemed humanity and the joyful sound of everlasting worship songs expressing glory to the Lamb.

These are the five reasons not to lose heart in Christian ministry:

By his mercy God has called you into his ministry.
Stand firm on the gospel and be faithful in your preaching.
Pray down the eye-opening ministry of the Holy Spirit.
God loves to use vulnerable people in his service to display his power.
Everything is a shadow of what is to come – the best is yet to be!

In the strength of the Lord, you can finish the race and complete the course.
Don't lose heart.

Originally prepared as a Palm Sunday sermon for a Christians Together in Torquay service in April 2011. It was subsequently used at a teaching day for the West of England Baptist Association Lay Ministries day in Bristol in September 2016.

The next two chapters are narrative sermons. Narrative preaching seeks to be faithful to a Bible passage but uses a story format as the form for the entire sermon.

8

A Hitchhiker's Guide to the Gospel

Acts 8:26-40

I work for the government civil service in the area of finance and banking. My country is very wealthy and a major trading centre in my part of the world. My boss is a woman; in fact, she is the wife of the king. In our Ethiopian culture, the affairs of State are considered too ordinary for the king, so he delegates this to his wife, and I am responsible for overseas trade missions.

Our country exports salt, ivory, gold, wine and we also have a lucrative trade in giraffes and elephants. Occasionally, trade missions involve me in travelling to other countries.

I am a religious man brought up in the Jewish tradition and, whenever possible, I like to visit the Temple in Jerusalem. I had been to the Temple and was returning home having purchased a scroll of Scripture to read during my journey. If I'm honest, I was not finding the passage an easy read and it was difficult to grasp its meaning.

As we travelled down the southern desert road, my driver spotted a hitchhiker in the distance. Now it may sound strange, but it's my habit to read aloud as my synagogue teacher had taught me. He said that some Scriptures were written for the ear, and you get a better understanding if you read aloud. The hitchhiker began running alongside my chariot and heard me reading aloud and he asked me, 'Do you understand what you are reading?'

I replied, 'I need someone to explain these words – why don't you join me?'

The hitchhiker sat alongside me, and I shared with him: 'These are the words I find puzzling:

"He was led like a sheep to the slaughter,
and as a lamb before its shearer is silent,
so he did not open his mouth.
In his humiliation he was deprived of justice.
Who can speak of his descendants?
For his life was taken from the earth."'

I asked the hitchhiker the question: 'Who is the writer talking about? Himself, or someone else?'

My hitchhiker friend, whose name was Philip, replied, 'Let me tell you about a man called Jesus.'

Now, I should add some background at this point because, while I was in Jerusalem the city had been on a high security alert. This religious prophet, Jesus, had been put to death a few months prior to my visit and there were rumours circulating that he was not dead. He had been seen alive by hundreds of people on separate occasions and there was a very tense atmosphere in the city.

There had been some violent clashes between the authorities and the growing numbers of followers of Jesus. The religious authorities had sanctioned the death of one of the leaders of the Jesus movement – a man called

Stephen who had been serving as one of their leaders had been stoned to death for blasphemy. Other followers had been arrested and put in prison and there had been a mass exodus of Jesus' followers from Jerusalem; many of them had travelled north to Samaria.

Now, I share this background with you to explain that when my hitchhiker friend said the name 'Jesus', this was not the first time I had heard his name. It was impossible to be a visitor to Jerusalem and not hear the name Jesus. After the business meetings of the day, over meals and late into the evening, everyone I spoke to had a viewpoint to share. The religious hardliners were delighted Jesus had departed and suggested he was a political radical and deserved to die. He was a rabble-rousing heretic who undermined the whole fabric of their faith. Many were convinced he was under the influence of the devil, saying, 'You can't have preachers publicly blaspheming the traditional faith. If you allow that, then the whole system would come tumbling down.'

But I met religious moderates who felt a deep sense of unease about Jesus' trial and conviction. Apparently Judge Pilate was reluctant to pass sentence and one of the soldiers guarding the crowds at the crucifixion site declared Jesus was an innocent man. These moderates found the simple lifestyle and story-telling wisdom of Jesus compelling. They were not signed-up followers of Jesus, but he had made them think differently about life. There was one businessperson I met who offered to introduce me to a relative who had been healed by Jesus. Another business associate invited me to a home group meeting where he said I could meet a man called Peter who knew Jesus personally. Sadly, I never accepted either of these invitations. But somewhere in all these conversations,

I discovered I had a fresh desire to study more carefully the Scriptures of my faith. Hence the purchase of the scroll of Scripture.

I am digressing – back to my hitchhiker friend, Philip. By a remarkable coincidence, he was one of the followers of Jesus. In fact, he had been recently appointed as part of the Jerusalem leadership team of seven men called deacons. He was a family man with four daughters who were all gifted speakers. Philip was the best-qualified teacher I could have met on my journey – I began to realise God must have sent him!

He started by telling me that I couldn't be studying a more important passage as I was reading from a book called the prophecy of Isaiah. Jesus had quoted more from Isaiah than any other book. Philip added: 'This is a book that helps you to understand more about Jesus.'

As we travelled south, we went through this Scripture passage line by line, and I had my questions ready for Philip. I asked him, 'Why do some people believe in this Jesus and others think he was deluded and dangerous?'

Philip pointed out the phrase in Isaiah, 'Who has believed our message and to whom has the arm of the LORD been revealed?' (53:1). He said the word 'revealed' means the significance of Jesus is like a secret that has to be discovered, and unless God shares the secret you will never discover it on your own. You won't discover the secret of Jesus by looking into his background, as this was very insignificant He was brought up in a poor family in Nazareth and quoted the well-known saying, 'Nothing significant ever comes from Nazareth'.[35] He said. 'You won't discover the secret by looking at his life, as outwardly Jesus

35. See John 1:46.

was very ordinary and unimpressive. He did not look like a King or sound like a world ruler. If you want to discover the secret of who Jesus is, then you have to ask God for the gift of faith and he will let you into the secret.'

My next question concerned the dark language of suffering in the passage I was reading. 'He was "despised and rejected"; "a man of sorrows",[36] full of grief.' I asked about these words, 'wounds', 'crushed' and 'pierced':[37] 'Who is the prophet referring to?'

Philip said these phrases were written by the prophet Isaiah 800 years before Jesus was born, but they could have been written by a reporter who was present on the day Jesus died on the cross. He told me they were a remarkably accurate account of a crucifixion when a condemned prisoner was wounded, crushed and pierced.

I know our Hebrew scriptures say: 'Anyone hanging on a tree is cursed by God.'[38] Therefore only sinners die a death as cruel as crucifixion. But Philip said this is the inner meaning of the cross! When Jesus was hanging on the tree, there was nothing wrong with his life. He was innocent of all sin but everything that was wrong was to do with our lives. Philip pointed out a simple phrase 'for our'. Jesus was 'wounded for our transgressions' and 'bruised for our iniquities'.[39] When he was dying on the cross, he was bearing our grief and carrying our sorrows.

Philip then told me a story. Apparently when Jesus was arrested and brought to trial, around the same time some Mafia-style criminals had also been arrested. They had been sentenced and were awaiting crucifixion and one

36. Isaiah 53:3, ESV.
37. Isaiah 53:5.
38. See Deuteronomy 21:23.
39. Isaiah 53:5, NKJV.

of those sentenced was a man called Barabbas. The first thing that happened to a convicted criminal after they'd been sentenced was, they had a visit from the prisoner carpenter. The carpenter's job was to measure a man for his cross and every convicted criminal was measured for the cross on which he would die. It was a cross tailor-made for him. So Barabbas had his own made-to-measure cross and it stood in the courtyard waiting to be carried by Barabbas to the place of execution.

Meanwhile Jesus had been arrested and his court trial was incredibly swift with no time for an appeal period that might lead to a reprieve. Judge Pilate even tried to release him because in his heart he knew Jesus was innocent, but he was fearful of what the religious leaders might do to destabilise an already volatile city. Pilate decided to evoke a custom where he could release a convicted prisoner and he brought out the hardened criminal Barabbas who had a terrible reputation as a murderer, and stood him alongside Jesus. He told the crowd he had the power to release one of these convicted men and made the crowd choose. 'Which one of these prisoners do you want me to release – Jesus or Barabbas?' Pilate expected the crowd to choose Jesus, but instead the crowd shouted more loudly for Barabbas! So Barabbas the murderer was released and Jesus the innocent was sent to the place of execution. There was no time for Jesus to be measured for his cross so when they came to the courtyard the soldiers gave Jesus the cross that had been measured for Barabbas and ordered him to carry that cross. Jesus was led by soldiers through the streets of Jerusalem to the place of execution, carrying the cross of Barabbas.

Barabbas was a free man and joined his cheering supporters in the crowd, and they decided to follow Jesus to see him crucified. Barabbas saw Jesus nailed to the cross and watched as the cross was lifted high and thudded into the socket in the ground. He then turned and said to his friends, 'That's my cross. That cross was measured for me. It should have been me hanging there.' Philip said this story of Barabbas would probably never find its way into the Holy Scriptures but it's a story with a powerful meaning.

I had one final question from the passage and returned to where I had begun. When the prophet Isaiah writes:

He was led like a sheep to the slaughter,
and as a lamb before its shearer is silent,
so he did not open his mouth.

I asked Philip: 'What is the significance of the silent lamb? Does this refer to Jesus as well?'

He replied that the more the disciples pondered on this verse from Isaiah, the more they came to realise there was one moment where this prophecy of Isaiah could apply to Jesus. It was a specific moment when Jesus was on trial before Judge Pilate, and as we have observed, the Judge was not convinced that Jesus deserved to die. He not only had his own misgivings, but his wife had experienced a disturbing dream, and she felt this was a warning and told her husband to have nothing to do with Jesus.[40]

Pilate did everything he could to release Jesus. But when the accusations came from the prosecution, to Pilate's dismay, Jesus offered no defence. He gave Pilate no answer to any of the charges brought. Jesus was as silent as a lamb. Philip said that when Jesus stood before Pilate on trial, it was a picture of every person standing before

40. See Matthew 27:19.

God, the righteous Judge. One day God will ask us to give an account of our lives and we will be asked whether we have loved God with all our heart, soul and mind. Have we believed and trusted Jesus for everything?

Our right response, said Philip, is to plead guilty and say nothing in our defence because we have not loved God wholly and not trusted Jesus, as we should. All we can do is to plead guilty – stay silent and cast ourselves on God's mercy.

Jesus had nothing to say to Pilate because we have nothing to say in our defence! When Jesus died on the cross, he was taking the sinners' place.

Philip then said to me that the disciples of Jesus had found it helpful to read this passage from Isaiah in a particular way. Instead of the central character remaining anonymous, they inserted the name of Jesus:

Jesus was wounded for our transgressions.
Jesus was bruised for our iniquities.
The chastisement on Jesus brought us peace.
My righteous servant Jesus through his suffering
will make many to be accounted righteous.

Then Philip added: 'And that includes you, my friend.' Things were beginning to fall into place and I did not need much more persuading. I asked Philip, 'Is there anything stopping me being baptised and becoming a follower of Jesus?' Philip replied that if I believed with all my heart that Jesus Christ is the Son of God, then I could become a follower.

I said, 'I do believe that Jesus Christ is the Son of God.' We stopped by a pool of water and there by the roadside Philip baptised me as I made my confession that Jesus is Lord. It was the best day of my life and a life-changing moment.

I never saw Philip again. As God brought him suddenly into my life, just as swiftly, he disappeared.

I returned home to my home country of Ethiopia, which is a long way from Jerusalem, so I had plenty of time on my journey to think how I was going to share my news with my friends and family.

I wondered how I would cope as a lone follower of Jesus, but I needn't have worried, as God was building his Church in my country and I was one of the first converts.

A few years went by and then one day, out of the blue, I received a parcel with a message from my friend Philip. The parcel contained a scroll of Scripture written by a friend of his called Luke, who had written two large books. One told the story of the earthly life of Jesus and the other was the history of the early years of the Church of Jesus. He had included in his second book the story of my encounter on the desert road.

In his letter to me, Philip shared he would have given a title for Luke's book and called it: 'A Hitchhikers Guide to the Gospel.'

I was invited by the Baptist Union of Scotland to address their annual Assembly at Glenrothes in October 2004. The organisers asked me to speak at six sessions on set passages from Luke's Gospel.

The only stipulation was they wanted my sermons to be in narrative format! This proved a challenge in preparation, but I greatly enjoyed this different style of preaching and have occasionally used this format.

I preached it again at the Baptist Assembly in Brighton in April 2006. The sermon on Zacchaeus was given the title 'The Inclusive Community'.

9

A Wealthy Man Meets Jesus

Luke 19:1-9

As a schoolboy I dreamt of being a rich man. It was one of my teachers who spotted I was good at maths and said: 'Zach, you will make a good businessman one day.' Boys in my class who were destined to be farmers may have counted sheep in their dreams, but I counted shekels.

When I was a young teenager, I looked around at the job options and broke my mother's heart when I said I wanted to join the Galilee tax service as a junior entrant. I said, 'Mother, give me one good reason why I shouldn't make tax collecting a career?'

She replied, 'My son, I will give you four good reasons why it's a bad choice. First, you will lose your friends. Second, you will get a bad reputation. Third, you will be barred from the synagogue and fourth you will break your dear mother's heart. Are you a good Jewish boy or not? Do you love your mama?'

It was a tough decision, but I went ahead anyway and joined the Tax Service and all my mother's predictions came true.

I *did* lose friends.

I *did* acquire a bad reputation.

I *was* barred from the synagogue.

And I *did* break my mother's heart.

But it was soon mended when I paid for her to have new furniture, gave her an annual summer holiday and presented her with five wonderful grandchildren.

I was fast-tracked through the Tax Service and within a few years was serving as the chief tax inspector for this region. It was a very lucrative job as I was making money from the people of Jericho, and I was taking a cut from the tax collectors who made money from the people. My boyhood dream had been fulfilled and I was a very wealthy man living in the beautiful town of Jericho. I had a new house built which overlooks the orchards of date palms. At night-time balsam groves produce the most wonderful smell of perfume. I married a wonderful wife, and we have some beautiful kids. We have the best furniture and there is never any shortage of food on the table.

But we were a lonely family, living isolated lives. Because of my work as tax collector, I was a hated man. Sometimes people spat on my wife when she was in the market and my children were bullied at school. My security bill was high as I paid to have my house guarded.

The neighbours are alright. Next door are the Abrahams – they own the largest furniture store in town – and across the street are the Josephs, who run the fruit stall in the market. Around the corner live the Balaams – they run the donkey stables. They have been in this business for centuries, but please don't make jokes about talking donkeys as they are quite sensitive about their family history. When we first moved in, the neighbours would not talk to us, but once they saw we were good customers, and

I recommended other wealthy tax collectors to do business with them, they changed their tune – and I came to an arrangement to give them tax relief.

As the chief inspector of the tax district, I do a fair amount of travelling visiting the toll booths on the major routes. It is here that I listen to people talking as they queue to go through the toll booths. This is when I first picked up the gossip about this travelling preacher called Jesus and the great crowds he was attracting. He was not only a great teacher, but he was performing many forms of healing miracles. Blind people had their sight restored and people who had been lame for years were able to walk. There were stories of him raising people from the dead and rumours he had attended a wedding where he turned water into wine.

But then there was the unusual story of my friend Matthew, who manages one of the tax booths further south. I got to know him when I attended one of the occasional tax conferences convened by the provincial administration when they update us on new legislation and price rises.

Apparently, this Jesus isn't fussy about who he chooses to mix with, and he had visited Matthew at his workplace and openly invited him to become one of his followers. Amazingly, Matthew immediately said 'Yes' to the invitation of Jesus, and his first response was to throw a dinner in his house for the staff in the local tax office, and he made Jesus the guest of honour. I can't remember the last time I heard of a rabbi visiting a tax collector's home!

Anyway, the word spread quickly that Jesus was coming to visit Jericho and curiosity made me join the large crowds that had begun to gather. By the time I got down to the main street, the crowds were three deep either side – and when you are my height there is no sense in beginning a fourth row. I looked up to the flat roofs of the houses on main street which were crowded with families looking down on the crowds below. Time was running out and Jesus would soon arrive – and I needed a vantage point.

Then I remembered the old tree in the town square. It was a sycamore tree with a short trunk and low branches. This was perfect for a grandstand view. I shinned up and sat on the first branch. It never occurred to me that I would be a sitting target for Jesus to spot me.

Don't ask me how he knew me. I can only assume that Matthew and his tax collector colleagues may have mentioned my name to Jesus. Perhaps they had suggested to Jesus, if he was passing through Jericho to 'look out for our friend Zacchaeus as he is one of the senior members of the tax collectors' union'. They might have added: 'You can't miss him as he is a small man and extremely wealthy.'

I nearly fell off the branch when Jesus came and stood under the tree and said, 'Zacchaeus, come down immediately. I must stay at your house today.'

You should have seen the faces of the neighbours when I walked down the street with Jesus. I saw the open mouths of the Abrahams family and the Joseph family standing in their doorways.

When we arrived at my home, I introduced the family to Jesus and then we went and sat in the balcony overlooking the date palms. It was the most open conversation I had ever had with anyone. To be honest, it was an enormous relief just to talk about life, about money and ambition. Especially about how to begin life again. It would have been easier if Jesus had suggested I moved away from Jericho and made a fresh start in a new community. If he had said to me, 'Leave everything, sell up and come on the road with me and become one of my travelling followers.' But Jesus indicated he liked some of his followers to stay where they were, in order to show to the community the power of a transformed life. By the end of Jesus' visit I was convinced I had to make an announcement. I had already agreed with Jesus what I would say publicly. I still have a copy of what I said to the crowd: 'As a result of Jesus' visit to my house and the honest conversation we have had, I have decided to give half of what I own to the poor of Jericho. Furthermore, I have decided that if I have defrauded anyone of anything, I will pay them back four times the amount I have wrongfully taken.'

Jesus was very supportive and said to the crowd that my promise was a sign of genuine repentance, and my proposed act of restitution made me a true relative of our great forefather Abraham. To silence any critics, he added: 'Zacchaeus is the kind of person I have come to meet and to save.'

Since meeting Jesus, my life has certainly been different. The people of Jericho were grateful to be compensated for their losses. Relationships are much easier with the neighbours. And my mother is overjoyed that I can now go to the synagogue with the family.

I receive the occasional invitation to share my story with house groups in nearby towns, and some of the more outgoing of these groups invite tax collectors for dinner to hear my story. But the strangest invitation came from a progressive group of Jesus followers who said my story of meeting Jesus had so inspired they were founding the Sycamore Society and were inviting me to be the patron. Their idea was to plant sycamore trees near the houses where they met each week. When anyone asked why they were planting sycamore trees, they simply shared my story! Every week they met in their homes to share the stories of Jesus, break bread together, and enjoy fellowship and prayers. They appeared to share their faith in Jesus very naturally with their neighbours and friends. They just talked about him. They thought I would like the strapline of the Sycamore Society:

Making it easy to meet Jesus!

This sermon was preached at a baptismal service at Upton Vale Baptist Church Torquay on 31 October 2021, when my friend Rob Irving was baptised.

I had journeyed with Rob as he attended two Alpha courses and then we both belonged to a micro group of four men called G4.

In 2000, I wrote a short book explaining the message of Romans.[41] One person has described a study of Romans as a spiritual blood transfusion for the local church.

In most centuries, the thinking of Christian leaders and their congregations has been shaped in profound ways by the teaching of this letter.

---

41. David Coffey, *Discovering Romans* (Leicester: Crossway Books, 2000).

10

Four Formidable Questions

Romans 8:28-39

It's a great privilege to be sharing in this baptismal service when my friend Rob will confess his faith in Jesus as Lord and Saviour. I can recall occasions when Rob and I would chat after a morning service, and he would share with me that he loved attending Upton Vale. He appreciated the songs that celebrated the Christian faith, the sermons that made him think, and the warm-hearted friends who made him feel at home in the church. But Rob would then share there hadn't been a light bulb moment for him. Despite the warm welcome, he felt he was an outsider looking in on something he didn't fully understand.

But as we shall hear in Rob's testimony, one day there was a light bulb moment – big time! As he was driving along the road to Paignton (not unlike the apostle Paul on the way to Damascus!), God appeared to him in an unmistakably special way and, as he drove, Rob made his personal commitment to be a follower of Jesus.

I cannot express fully the joy it gives me to have observed at close hand the slow process in Rob's spiritual journey of faith. Two years ago, Rob was married to Kirstin, and a baptism day in some respects is like a wedding day. Wedding days are full of joy and confidence, and you hear warm-hearted vows which express love and commitment. But a wedding day is also a day of ice-cold reality which is reflected in the wedding vows: 'For better, for worse, for richer, for poorer, in sickness and in health.'[42]

A baptism day is similar. It is a day of warm vows, expressing love and commitment to God but it's also a day of ice-cold reality. We don't use the wedding vows at a baptismal service, but we could. We could ask Rob today the question:

Do you promise to follow Jesus as Lord for ever –
For better for worse, for richer for poorer, in sickness and in health?

Every disciple of Jesus coming to be baptised is invited to make warm-hearted vows of love and commitment knowing that someday they will be challenged by some ice-cold questions:

Is God really for me?
Is he truly on my side?
In the face of everything that life is throwing at me,
can I be absolutely sure that God's love for me
is utterly trustworthy and reliable
and that nothing will ever separate me from the love of God?

---

42. Christopher J. Ellis and Myra Blyth, *Gathering for Worship-Patterns and Prayers for the Community of Disciples* (Norwich: Canterbury Press 2005), p. 207.

These may appear as bleak questions on a day of great joy, but commitment and conflict, doubt and discipleship are close partners. Remember the Bible says that immediately after Jesus was baptised, he spent forty long days in the desert being tempted by Satan. The devil quizzed Jesus about whether God's love could be trusted, and he was tempted about the reliability of God's love. The Bible passage this morning faces some formidable questions about the love of God. Romans chapter 8:28-39 are among the most famous verses in the Bible that address this question: Can I be sure of God's love for me?

It has been said that reading the book of Romans is like being swept along in a small boat on a fast-flowing river. So, sit tight if you are going to stay on board! Romans is a challenging book of sixteen chapters and chapter 8 is the halfway mark and the high point in the book, often called the Mount Everest of Romans.

Paul has been sharing about God's love revealed in the life, death and resurrection of Jesus and as he approaches the summit, he shares how the Holy Spirit comes to do in our lives all that Jesus has done for us through his death on the cross (vv. 1-17). But then Paul suddenly stops climbing and addresses his readers with a question: 'What [can] we say in response to all these things?' (v. 31, AMP).

What does Paul mean by 'all these things?' The 'all things' are in the verses preceding and can be summed up in three words – suffering, weakness and groaning (vv. 18-27). There are sufferings in the Christian life and becoming a Christian is not an insurance policy making you immune to the bad things that can happen. Becoming a disciple means you sign up for suffering, weakness and groaning. We live in a fallen world where the whole of creation is in discord. People suffer, and the creation groans with pain.

But there is good news in Romans 8. One day Jesus Christ will return to earth and the day of climate conferences will be over. God will create a new heaven and a new earth, and it will be a revelation of God's glory. The 'present sufferings are not worth comparing with the glory that will be revealed' (vv. 18-22).

But in this in-between time, there are times of great suffering. The sufferings we experience are so heavy a burden there are moments in our weakness when we don't know what to pray. So, we resort to just groaning – 'O my God' – and amazingly the Holy Spirit takes the groans of our suffering and translates them into prayers. Nothing is lost in translation. These prayers are heard by Jesus, our friend in high places. Jesus co-suffers with us when we are weak and his heart is drawn towards our suffering, weakness and groaning with pain.

But these experiences are the very things that provoke the big questions of life. Romans 8:28 sounds wonderfully confident: 'And we know that in all things God works for the good of those who love him, who have been called according to his purpose.' But when we are suddenly faced with suffering weakness and groaning, we begin to question:

Is God really working for my good in all things?
Can I be sure that God is in control of events?
Will there ever be a conclusion to the chaos in my life?

To answer these questions we need to think like gospel people. The gospel is basically everything that Jesus did and said and it's called good news. Thinking the gospel is allowing the central truths of the faith to address the harsh events of life. It means you stand all the suffering, groaning and weakness in front of the gospel story of Jesus and let it speak to you. This is what Paul does here. He stands his personal experience of suffering, groaning and weakness in front of the gospel story and asks four formidable questions:

Question 1

'If God is for us, who can be against us?' (v. 31)

Who is this God who is for us? First, he is the God who made you. The BBC programme *Who Do You Think You Are?* is running a new series which will be watched by millions. It is very moving when a Josh Widdicombe or a Dame Judi Dench discover something which has remained hidden in their ancestry.

The Bible asks the same question: *Who do you think you are?* If we are willing to do the research, we will discover the Bible says we are uniquely created in God's image. Ephesians 2:10 says we are 'God's handiwork, created in Christ Jesus to do good works, which God prepared in advance for us to do'. We are not products from a human assembly line where everyone looks and sounds the same. You are made in God's image as a unique 'you'.

I am a unique David Coffey. When I went for my Covid-19 vaccination last week, I arrived at the desk to hear one nurse say to the other nurse, 'I am dying for a coffee.' And I said, 'Well, here I am! My name is Coffey!' Each of us is unique, and because God created you, he knows you personally. There is a wonderful passage of poetic brilliance in the book of Psalms. In Psalm 139 the writer describes just how *well* God knows you. These are the opening lines in *The Message*:

157

GOD, investigate my life;
get all the facts firsthand.
I'm an open book to you;
even from a distance, you know what I'm thinking.
You know when I leave and when I get back;
I'm never out of your sight.
You know everything I'm going to say
before I start the first sentence.
I look behind me and you're there,
then up ahead and you're there, too –
your reassuring presence, coming and going.
This is too much, too wonderful –
I can't take it all in!

The God who made you is for you and if God is for you, who can be against you! The God who made you and understands you has promised he will never abandon what he has made. Believing this truth doesn't answer all the questions about suffering, but you must trust that the God who made you and knows you is for you – and above all loves you, which is why he sent Jesus to earth to demonstrate to the full how much he loves us.

God didn't hesitate to spare his own Son, Jesus (v. 32), and he exposed himself to the worst of suffering on the cross. God has given us everything in Jesus and this is the pledge of his love.

It is this God who is working in all things for our good (v. 28), so if this God is on our side, how can we be losers?

There are two more formidable questions about God's love in verses 33-34.

Question 2

'Who will bring any charge against those God has chosen?'

Question 3

'Who . . . is the one who condemns [a believer]?'

In The Message version of this passage, it says: 'And who would dare tangle with God by messing with one of God's chosen? Who would dare even to point a finger?' Paul is thinking of those moments when you suffer inwardly even after becoming a Christian. There are those moments when you do something so terrible that you begin to doubt if God could still love you. Satan piles in to condemn and accuse us and says: 'And you are meant to be a Christian?' Paul imagines a courtroom scene where Satan attempts to put believers on trial with charges full of condemnation. Satan is an expert in provoking guilt and shame, even in the lives of the saintliest Christian. It is a warning to anyone being baptised. For the rest of your life, Satan will attempt to resurrect things from the past. Things to make you blush with shame. He charges us – condemns us – accuses us. How can God possibly love someone has wretched as you? This is the moment the counsel for the defence asks: 'Who is daring to tangle with one of God's chosen? Who dares to point a finger at this disciple?'

Counsel for the defence of the disciple is Jesus, the mighty Saviour who defeated Satan on the cross. The final nail in Satan's coffin was Jesus rising from the dead. The last words of Jesus to his disciples before he ascended to heaven was: 'All authority in heaven and on earth has been given to me . . .' (Matthew 28:18-20). This implies Jesus is saying: 'I am the chief executive officer of the universe.' This is the God who is for you, standing there to defend you against all the condemnation. He shows Satan, the accuser, the nail marks in his blood-stained hands and proclaims: 'You have no power to condemn this saint, who belongs to Jesus!'

Question 4

'[Is there anything that can] separate us from the love of Christ?' (v. 35)

Paul mentions some of the things that might separate us from the love of Christ. Is it possible that the experience of trouble, hardship, persecution might separate us? Paul says he is absolutely convinced that nothing can separate him from God's love. How can Paul be so confident there is nothing that can separate us from God's love?

First, because of his experiences. He lists some of the sufferings he has experienced in the New Testament letter called 2 Corinthians and in chapter 11. Paul lists some of the things he suffered as a Christian. Consider the list:

Paul was beaten, stoned and shipwrecked.
Eight times he says, 'my life was in danger',
'Danger in the city' – 'danger in the country' – 'danger at sea'.
There were people who wanted to kill him.
There were storms at sea that threatened to destroy him.
When the population of Ephesus attempted to silence his preaching,
he said it was like fighting with 'wild beasts' (1 Corinthians 15:32).

In none of these situations did Paul feel he was separated from God's love. It is always worth listening to someone's personal testimony of experiencing the love of God. But more important than his personal experience is his confidence in Jesus Christ. The fear we sometimes have as believers is that the rawness of our painful suffering will be so great, it will separate us from the love of God. That our hold on God will not be strong enough. Jesus is the guarantee that nothing will separate us from God's love. In a few weeks we will celebrate Christmas and share again the story of the birth of Jesus. Do you remember how Mary and Joseph were told what name to give their baby? They were told to call him Jesus, 'because he will save his people from their sins' (Matthew 1:21).

This baby Jesus was destined to die thirty-three years after his birth. He was born to be a Saviour who would die on the cross. This was God's plan and purpose for his beloved Son. Think for a moment of all the occasions when Jesus could have walked away from this calling on his life.

He could have given in to Satan's temptations in the wilderness.
He could have compromised with religious leaders of the day.
He could have walked out of Gethsemane saying, 'I can't drink this cup.'
He could have said to Pilate 'I apologise for wasting your time – I'm not a king.'
In those final moments, hanging on the cross, betrayed by Judas, denied by Peter, deserted by his disciples,
finally forsaken by God in the midnight of the cross – Jesus could have called on God to rescue him from the suffering on the cross.
But he stayed there.
He stayed there because he loved you!

It is never how strong is my love for God. It is always how strong is his love for me. The cross is the measure of how much God loves us. That is why God's Word says, there is nothing, absolutely nothing that can 'separate us from the love of God that is in Christ Jesus our Lord'.

You take your suffering and your doubts and stand them in front of these four formidable questions on God's love:

If God is for us, who can be against us?
Who is there to condemn us?
Who can bring any charges against those whom God has chosen?
Is there anything that can separate us from the love of Christ?

There are some things in life we don't know. And there are some things we will never know. But here is one thing we do know. Romans 8:28 says, 'we know that in all things God is working for the good of those who love him, who have been called according to his purpose'.

It is the greatest thing in life to be in the company of those who have been called by God.

Remember, you did not choose the Lord, he chose you. And this God is *for* you!

I was invited to preach at the church anniversary of Whetstone Baptist Church, Leicester in November 2022.

The congregation had been worshipping in their new premises, known as Springwell, for just over a year.

I served as the pastor of Whetstone from 1967-72. It was my first pastorate and Janet and I had only been married a year. So I was a rookie husband and pastor! Our children, Niki and Phil, were both born in Leicester, and Janet and I will always be grateful for the support and encouragement we received from this church fellowship.

I believe the foundation stones for my future ministry were laid firmly during my time serving this church. It was a particular joy to renew fellowship with those I knew as teenagers, who are still following the Lord as grandparents!

In preparing this sermon I found great help in reading Darrell W. Johnson's book *Who is Jesus?* (Vancouver: Regent College Publishing, 2011).

David, Janet, Niki and Phil. Whetstone, 1972

11

The Power of Jesus

Mark 1:14-28

For a few years I was regularly commuting between Didcot, Oxfordshire and Washington DC. The late evening British Airways flight from Washington to Heathrow is known as the 'Red Eye'. The flight departs Washington Dulles at 10:30 in the evening and lands you in London Heathrow around eleven in the morning.

Thirty years ago, I was on that Red Eye flight and on the way to the departure gate, I dropped into the airport bookshop and asked the assistant if she could recommend a paperback. She suggested a new book by Thomas Harris. Around midnight I picked up the paperback and for the first time I noticed the title: *The Silence of the Lambs*.[43]

The title didn't mean anything to me, as the Oscar-winning film starring Jodie Foster and Anthony Hopkins was yet to be released. The main thing I recall about reading the paperback was how terrified I was to turn the page to discover what dreadful atrocities Hannibal Lecter

---

43. Thomas Harris, *The Silence of the Lambs* (NY: St Martin's Press, 1988).

had committed! In the film version of the book, Jodie Foster plays Clarice Starling, the rookie FBI officer who visits Hannibal Lecter in prison. The prison governor warns Starling about the potential of Hannibal the Cannibal crawling round inside her head. The governor tells her Hannibal Lecter is a monster.

When we are faced with unspeakable evil in the world, what questions do we ask? When we read the court trial accounts of a hospital nurse accused of murdering babies in her care, or watch a harrowing documentary of suspected war crimes perpetrated in Ukraine, do we reach for the word 'evil'?

This morning our Bible passage sees the power of Jesus in action. We read what happened when his powerful preaching aroused the powers of evil. But the first thing to note about Jesus is:

1. The power of his calling (vv. 14-20)

The preaching ministry of John the Baptist has prepared the way for Jesus (Mark 1:1-8). Jesus now comes preaching the good news of God and there is an urgency about his preaching. In verse 15 Jesus says: 'The time has come'. The world has waited centuries for this moment to arrive. One of the great themes of the Old Testament is: 'The time will come when the true king visits earth and launches his kingdom.' That time has come!

Jesus' preaching has a very basic message (v. 15):

The kingdom of God has come near.
Repent and believe the good news.

166

In other words, 'Turn round from the way you have been living and follow me.'

In a world where there are many religions offering good advice, the unique feature of the Christian faith is it offers good news. Other religions suggest there is something you can do to live the good life. The gospel message is something has been done! Jesus Christ lived and died and rose again to bring us home to God. This is the good news and Jesus calls us to believe it.

We see the power of Jesus as people respond to his calling. As Jesus is walking by the Sea of Galilee, a major centre for the fishing industry, Jesus sees two men fishing from a boat. He calls out to Peter and his brother Andrew: 'Come, follow me . . . and I will send you out to fish for people' (v. 17). Immediately they left their jobs as fishermen and became followers of Jesus.

Jesus continues his walk by the fishing boats and spots two more fishermen in a boat. They were twin brothers, James and John, who had a reputation for violent tempers, which is probably why Jesus gave them the nickname 'Boanerges', which means 'sons of thunder' (Mark 3:17). There is no explanation why Jesus gave them this nickname, but there are episodes in the Gospels where we read of the twins' impetuous responses to a situation facing the disciples.

When the power of Jesus' call comes to your life, the first thing is *the calling is personal*. He calls you by name to be a follower, and this is unique. Remember, in the first century, you were the one with the power to choose. You chose your favourite rabbi and requested to be a follower of a particular teacher. With Jesus it is different, which is why Jesus says: 'You did not choose me, but I chose you [to] go and bear fruit – fruit that will last' (John 15:16). In your testimony you can say you have decided to follow

Jesus. But remember this is only possible in response to his calling. You can't have a relationship with Jesus until you are called by him.

A friend of mine is a taxi driver in his late fifties and a new follower of Jesus who was recently baptised. His testimony is Jesus was calling him for many years but unwisely he chose to ignore the call. He now realises Jesus was calling him personally and one of his deepest regrets is he didn't respond sooner. Norman is now making up for lost time and God is using his taxi service to enable him to be a good news missionary on four wheels!

The second thing to note is Jesus always calls people with a *purpose in mind.* His purpose for the first four disciples was they would stop landing fish for the market stalls and start catching people for the kingdom. Jesus will take them out of their narrow world of fishing and launch them into a much bigger world of mission.

Peter would discover his calling as a preacher and his preaching would confound the experts. They would query how a rural fisherman who had never been to college could speak with such spiritual authority (Acts 4:13). Answer – it's the power of Jesus' calling.

Andrew would discover his calling as a missionary and his travels would take him to the borders of Russia, that area north of the Black Sea where the ruthless Barbarians ruled. How was a humble fisherman transformed into travelling missionary? Answer – it's the power of Jesus' calling.

James, and his brother, John, egged on by their mother, were aggressively ambitious. Their mother approached Jesus with her sons and had the gall to ask him for reserved seats for her boys when Jesus came into his kingdom (Matthew 20:20-28). In Mark's Gospel, it is James and John who approach Jesus with the request about privileged seating. Jesus suggests they have no idea what they are asking. He questions whether they can drink the cup of suffering which he is about to face. It will be like a baptism of death in that he will be fully immersed in suffering on the cross (Mark 10:35-40).

John had the gifts of a loving pastor and a gifted writer. He endured exile on the Island of Patmos where the Lord gave him visions which we now possess as the last book in the Bible. He ended his ministry as the Bishop of Ephesus and was renowned as 'the one Jesus loved' (John 20:2).

You get the message. The power of Jesus' calling takes you out of a narrow world and places you in a world of wider purpose. He might call you to Mexico – which is where the call took my friends Helen and Steve Cosslett. God might call you to Guinebor II Hospital in Chad, which is where my pharmacist friend Claire Bedford is working with BMS[44] World Mission.

God may call you to blossom right where you are. Not a change of location but a change of attitude. But when he calls, follow him – and let the adventures begin.

In the next verses you see:

2. The power of Jesus' preaching (vv. 21-22)

Jesus and his four new disciples go to the synagogue in Capernaum. It was the Sabbath day and the usual congregation had gathered:

Fishermen and their families.
Builders and their relatives.
Market stall people and their friends.

---

44. BMS: Baptist Missionary Society.

As Jesus began to teach, the people were amazed. The meaning behind the Greek 'amazed' is a strong word. It means physically struck with awe and shock. Today we might say they were gobsmacked. Why? Because Jesus taught with personal authority.

You see, every Sabbath the congregation would listen to traditional preachers and all these traditional preachers did was to quote other preachers. They would say Rabbi John says this, but on the other hand you might be interested to know Rabbi Gamaliel has made this comment. And if you really want to go deep then I recommend you check out what Rabbi Malachi says on this passage.

You can imagine the local builder walking home from the synagogue and saying to his wife, 'All this quoting rabbis is doing my head in. I may not come to the synagogue service next week. I may just turn up at the end for the tea and coffee!'

Jesus didn't quote dusty old rabbis. Unlike the sermon he preached in his hometown of Nazareth (Luke 4:14-30), we don't have the precise content of Jesus' sermon, but we do know the familiar pattern of Jesus' teaching. It would be along these lines: Jesus would say: 'You have heard it said – but I say.' Those three words, 'but I say' – a congregation would not hear from the lips of a traditional rabbi.

For example, Jesus said, 'You have heard it said – do not murder. *But I say* – anyone who is angry will be subject to God's judgement.'

'You have heard it said – love your friends and hate your enemies. *But I say* – love your enemies and pray for those who persecute you.'

No wonder the congregation was gobsmacked! This is the unique authority of Jesus, both then and now. Remember, this is God in Christ visiting the earth as a preacher. The

God who said in Genesis 1:3, '"Let there be light," and there was light', is the preacher in the Capernaum synagogue on a Sabbath day shedding the light of his Word in the dark places of the heart.

The preacher will be speaking to your heart in Springwell this morning. The Word of God is described as 'alive and active. Sharper than any doubled-edged sword' (Hebrews 4:12). It is like a surgeon's scalpel, able to cut through to the heart of the matter. Every time you hear the gospel story, feel the power of Jesus preaching into your own life. When he says: 'If anyone is spiritually thirsty, let him to come to me and drink and out of him will flow rivers of living water' (see John 7:27-38) – respond swiftly to his invitation. When Jesus says: 'Come to me, all who are labouring with heavy burdens, and I will give you rest' (see Matthew 11:28) – open your heart to feel the power of those words and respond to his kind invitation.

We need more congregations to be 'amazed' at the preaching of Jesus through his servants!

The path to being amazed is realising afresh that when God's Word is opened, I am expected to listen humbly and obey promptly.

A little girl during the morning service at her church was presented with a new Bible. It was the prize for a competition she had won. After the service, an older member congratulated her on her prize and asked if she could see the new Bible. The girl handed it over, but then said, 'Don't open it. If you open the Bible, you will let God out!'

That's why when we open the Word each Sunday, it lets God out and we experience his transforming power.

We have seen the power of Jesus' call, and the power of his preaching. The final thing to observe in the passage is the Power of his authority.

3. The power of Jesus' authority (vv. 23-28)

As Jesus was preaching, all hell breaks loose in the synagogue. His powerful preaching has disturbed the world of demons. A man possessed by an evil spirit shrieks out at the top of his voice: 'What have you to do with us, Jesus of Nazareth? Have you come to destroy us?' The shouting is full of aggression: 'You have no business here, Jesus. This is our world.'

We need to read this encounter with Satan in the wider context of Jesus' life. From the moment the baby Jesus is born in Bethlehem, Satan wants him destroyed. He uses the madness of King Herod to massacre baby boys in Bethlehem, but Jesus escapes the satanic slaughter of the innocents. Joseph is warned in a midnight dream to get out of Bethlehem and take his wife and new-born baby and escape to Egypt (Matthew 2:13-18). If he doesn't escape immediately, then Herod will search for Jesus to kill him. Herod was clearly possessed by a satanic spirit.

The Bethlehem Satan now appears as Satan in the synagogue. There must have been a deathly silence in the synagogue as the congregation wait to see what the preacher will do. Look at the power of Jesus' authority. Jesus rebukes the evil spirit in the man. With awesome authority he commands: 'Shut up and get out.'

Convulsing the man and shrieking loudly, the evil spirit came out of him. Shouting with a great shout, the man is set free from Satan's power. The shocked congregation respond for the second time. 'What's this? First, preaching with authority. Now he commands the evil spirits, and they obey him' (see v. 27). No wonder the news about Jesus spread like wildfire!

Now pause and reflect on what we have read. This passage from Mark's Gospel is more than a first-century story about Jesus. The power of Jesus' authority is desperately needed for our broken world today. But how do we interpret this story of satanic possession? In our sophisticated world with its understanding of psychiatry and psychology, how are we going to apply the teaching of this passage? We face an imposing challenge when we encounter the Western mind where everything that happens has a human cause and a scientific explanation.

I find Darrell Johnson helpful at this point. How you understand this story in Mark 1 will depend on your world view. He draws attention to the secular view being a simple two-dimensional view of life. There is me and my life, and there is the world around me.[45]

The best example of this two-dimensional thinking is the political chaos of the last few months. The tumultuous events of the world around me had suddenly impacted my life. The up and down roller coaster of the financial markets, fed by some foolish political decisions, has aroused fears and uncertainty about mortgages, pensions, savings and the viability of future employment. The human tragedy that unravelled after Russia invaded Ukraine left thousands of people uprooted from their homes fleeing the terrors of war and seeking refuge in other countries.

The world has always had to live with political chaos and evil dictators, but the Bible worldview is never two-dimensional. It is four-dimensional:

There is me.
There is the physical world.
There is the living God who is always active in the world he made and loves.
And there is the world of unseen evil spiritual powers.

---

45. Darrell Johnson, *Who is Jesus?* (Vancouver: Regent College Publishing, 2011), pp. 84-85.

The Bible is clear. You will never fully understand life if you persist in living in a two-dimensional world. As Christian disciples we take seriously the four-dimensional world. Ephesians 6 is the Bible passage that makes plain how twenty-first century disciples are to interpret Mark 1:

Put on the full armour of God, so you can take your stand against the devil's schemes. For our struggle is not against flesh and blood, but against the rulers, against the authorities, against the powers of this dark world and against the spiritual forces of evil in the heavenly realms.'
(Ephesians 6:10-12)

You will certainly experience moments in life when you know you are battling against the spiritual forces of evil. This is why you are commanded to dress yourself in the spiritual armour God provides (Ephesians 6:13-18).

Please don't walk out of Springwell this morning to live as a two-dimensional human relying on human power and ingenuity to see you through the battles of life. God intends you to live — not by power or might, but by his Spirit (Zechariah 4:6)!

As Darrell Johnson reminds us, there is no sphere of life where the powerful authority of Jesus cannot overrule. And there is no predicament you may fall into where the power of Jesus cannot rescue you.

That Sabbath day in the synagogue Jesus demonstrated his power and authority over evil. A poor victim of Satan was rescued and delivered. As we read through Mark and study the ministry of Jesus, we see Satan repeatedly returning to the fight. He is bent on destroying Jesus and his followers. He attempted to kill the baby Jesus in Bethlehem and his final attempt to kill Jesus is on the cross.

Come and stand on Calvary in the dying embers of the first Good Friday.

Listen to the shrieks of the demons as the nails are hammered into the hands of Jesus.

It appears Satan has at last claimed a final victory for evil. Jesus dies.

But then a series of extraordinary things begin to happen after the death of Jesus. In the Jerusalem Temple the giant curtain, 60ft high and 30ft wide, is torn in two from top to bottom. There has already been a mid-afternoon darkness lasting three hours and now there is an earthquake. As the earth shakes, rocks are split apart and graves are opened – and many holy people who had died and been buried were raised to life, and after the resurrection of Jesus they came out of their tombs and went into the city and 'appeared to many people' (Matthew 27:51-53).

Why are these events recorded in the Gospel? They are clear signs that death and the devil have been defeated. Through the death of Jesus, Satan has been robbed of his greatest weapon, namely death. Jesus lives and is alive for evermore!

On numerous occasions I have been with a grieving family at a crematorium. It is a day of great sorrow. Surrounded by unending grief and brokenness of heart, which will not be healed in an instant, I am thankful that I am able to speak those ancient scriptural words of comfort, defyingly triumphant words in the face of sudden death:

Where, O death, is your victory?
Where, O death, is your sting?
. . . Thanks be to God! He gives us the victory through our Lord Jesus Christ.

(1 Corinthians 15:55-57)

You have seen the power of Jesus' calling.
Has he called you and are you following him?
Are you blossoming where he has placed you?
You have seen the power of Jesus' preaching.
As the word is opened, do you hear the Lord speaking to you?
Do you respond to the invitations of his Word?
You have seen the power of Jesus' authority.
Can you say: 'Thank you, Lord, there is no sphere of life where your power cannot rule, and there is no predicament I may fall into where your power cannot rescue me'?
Now, go out into the world bearing this promise:

To him who is able to do immeasurably more than all we ask or imagine, according to his power that is at work within us, to him be glory in the church and in Christ Jesus throughout all generations, for ever and ever! Amen.
(Ephesians 3:20-21)

This sermon was prepared for the induction of Steve Cosslett as an associate pastor at Upton Vale on 12 January 2020.

But the day before the service I lost my voice and was unable to preach or even attend the service.

Instead, our senior pastor, Andy Hickford, chose to read my sermon verbatim. This was the first experience I had of preparing a sermon that would be delivered by another preacher.

I was told by those who were present that Andy read it such a way that the congregation could 'hear' my voice!

The service had a special significance as thirty-eight years previously I had dedicated Steve as a baby.

12

The Duties of a Minister

2 Timothy 4:1-8

I read recently the results of an online survey on what people expect from perfect pastors, and I thought it was appropriate to share this on Steve's induction Sunday.

The list of perfection included the following:

Perfect pastors preach for exactly twelve minutes.
They are twenty-eight years of age.
They are very good-looking.
They work from 8 a.m. until midnight every day.
They frequently condemn sin but manage never to upset anyone.

I've never trusted online surveys – especially those concerning perfect pastors!

Many of you will realise that this is a very special day for Steve and myself. On the 8 August 1982, Stephen Christopher Cosslett was brought by his parents, Larry and Chris, to be dedicated to God and his service. I conducted that service and thirty-eight years later I am sharing in a service where we are dedicating Steve to his ministry here at Upton Vale. I can only say: Thanks be to God for fulfilling the prayers of faith offered over Steve as a child.

This morning in our series in 2 Timothy we are studying 2 Timothy 4:1-8 and I want to take a phrase Paul uses in his advice to a young pastor called Timothy, and then explain from the passage how Pastor Tim was expected to conduct his life as a pastor. The phrase is this: 'Discharge all the duties of your ministry' (v. 5).

From this passage we see the first duty is to fear the Lord.

1. Fear the Lord (v. 1)

Paul begins by reminding Timothy that all ministry is conducted in the sight of God.

Before he outlines the duties of a pastor, he states that the advice he is about to offer – what he calls a 'charge' – is under the survey of God Almighty: 'In the presence of God and of Christ Jesus, who will judge the living and the dead, and in view of his appearing and his kingdom, I give you this charge' (v. 1).

These are very solemn words, and they are a reminder that the first duty is to fear the Lord. Every feature of our work is conducted in the presence of God and of his Christ Jesus.

The Greek word for appearing is *epiphany*. In the Church calendar since Christmas, we are in the season of Epiphany, when we remember the appearing of Christ to the wise men. They had travelled hundreds of miles, drawn by a mysterious moving star, and eventually arrived in Bethlehem. There, revealed to them, was a baby lying in the manger who had been declared by angels to be the Saviour of the whole world. Thirty years later when Jesus began his ministry of signs and wonders, he announced the arrival of God's kingdom on earth. Our ministry as pastors is conducted in the light of this appearing and this kingdom!

Jesus has once appeared, and he will appear again on earth when he comes as the King of glory and the righteous judge. He appeared in Bethlehem as the Saviour of the world and announced in Nazareth that God's kingdom has broken into our world. His appearing and his kingdom are the bedrock realities of our ministry – and for this reason we fear the Lord.

The Message version of this passage underlines the solemnity of Paul's words:

> I can't impress this on you too strongly. God is looking over your shoulder. Christ himself is the Judge, with the final say on everyone, living and dead.

Why does Paul lay this solemn charge at Timothy's door? Because if, as a pastor, you fail to make it a priority to fear God, then you will end by fearing people.

I commenced my ministry in Leicester in 1967 when I was a young twenty-six-year-old pastor who had been married just a year to my beautiful young bride, aged twenty-four. Janet and I knew very little about life, marriage or pastoring a church. Is it any wonder that I feared the elders, and the deacons and I feared the congregation. I retained a particular fear for some of the most fearful members!

On my final Sunday, when I had preached my last sermon before moving to North Cheam Surrey, one of the fearsome members said to me: 'David, you haven't preached many bad sermons while you've been our minister, but tonight was one of them!'

From personal experience, I am sharing that you can never discharge the duties of your ministry, if you fear the people. A healthy church is where everyone fears the Lord and all our service begins in the presence of God and Christ Jesus.

This makes this induction service a solemn charge (v. 1). As Tom Wright comments on these verses:

> Paul has lived his life with God's clock ticking in the background. Jesus is already enthroned as king of the world and one day we shall see his royal appearing – the time when the whole world will be held to account.[46]

The Judge and his kingdom are the bedrock realities that motivate us as ministers.

We begin by fearing the Lord. There can never be a culture of self-centeredness in the ministry, because we serve a God who says in his Word: 'Christ died that we may 'no longer live for [ourselves] but for him who . . . died and [rose from the dead]' (2 Corinthians 5:15, ESV).

Some aspects of our ministry can be likened to life on a stage, where the most important person in the audience is the Living God. So I urge you, Steve, listen first for his applause and his affirmation.

The second duty of your ministry is to:

---

46. Tom Wright, *Paul for Everyone: The Pastoral Letters: 1 and 2 Timothy and Titus* (London: SPCK, 2003), p. 124.

2. Preach the Word (v. 2)

A new minister to a church received a letter from a former pastor who wished him well and offered this advice:

> As you pastor this church,
> you will need the courage of a lion,
> the skin of a rhinoceros,
> the wisdom of an owl,
> the patience of a polar bear,
> and if there is an animal with eyes in the back of
> the head,
> this could also prove useful.

I am confident the Upton Vale ministry team collectively is a menagerie of talent with an ample supply of courage, wisdom and patience! Paul's wisdom is simply to 'preach the word'.

Paul adds: 'Be prepared [to do this] in and out of season' (v. 2). In other words, preach God's Word whenever the opportunity arises. The faithful minister speaks the Word in and out of the pulpit, in the home and in the workplace. For this task of preaching the Word you will need the help of the Holy Spirit because, as Dave Hansen observes: 'The human heart is the most fiercely guarded piece of ground in the universe.'[47]

As a sermon progresses a congregation begins to divide. Some will be comforted but others will resist. People protect their hearts like a heavily guarded fortress, and wise pastors know that preachers don't gain entrance into the citadel of the heart that easily. That's why we pray as

47. David Hansen, *The Art of Pastoring: Ministry Without All the Answers* (Downers Grove, IL: IVP, 1994), p. 99.

we preach: 'Lord, let your Holy Spirit be at work changing lives as I preach your Word.'

I would remind us, as a church family, that preaching is never a performance. We don't watch the preacher as an audience. Preaching is a participation because there are always three persons in the pulpit. The preacher, the Holy Spirit and the author of the book – in this case, Paul. This trinity of persons are working to communicate the message God has for his people. As his people, our work is to listen carefully, and then obey.

The congregation must become accustomed to the different styles of preaching. There will be times of challenge, warning and encouragement. But the preacher must always do his work of communicating with 'great patience and careful instruction' (v. 2). In other words, when the congregation don't get the message first time, the preacher patiently explains the same truth next week. Preaching the word is more than passing on information.

We preach to transform lives. We preach to change people.
I say to all our preachers at Upton Vale:
Preach the story of Jesus – and ask God to open the eyes of the blind.
Preach the comforting words of Scripture.
Preach the wise words of Scripture that will equip the mind.
Because people are drawn by strange ideas, preach to correct errors.
Because people are careless with their lives, preach to expose sin.
Because people become discouraged, preach to encourage perseverance.

Preach so that people are taught to walk like Jesus walked.

3. Guard the faith (vv. 3-5)

In many places Paul says to younger Timothy that he is to 'guard what has been entrusted to your care' (1 Timothy 6:20; see also 2 Timothy 1:12). Why is the duty of guarding the faith so important? Paul gives his reasons in verses 3-5.

> There will come a time when people tolerate sound teaching.
> They will get itchy ears only wanting to hear their favourite doctrine.
> They will hunt down teachers who will scratch their itchy ears.

People get itchy ears over how the world began and how it will end. They get itchy ears over Bible prophecy and the Middle East today. They get itchy ears over issues of human sexuality. Andy has my full support for his current series on 'A Better Story – God's word casting light on issues of human sexuality'. Pray for him as he preaches the word to the cultures of the day!

It is essential for the health of the church fellowship that pastors defend the faith. Good ministers defend the faith and grow healthy congregations where there is no sickness of speculation and no fever of deviation.

4. Develop your character (v. 5)

Some parts of ministry are not to do with using great gifts and talents. The duty of ministry is also about developing a Christlike character that supports the great gifts. Paul's clear advice to Timothy is to keep his head in all situations and endure hardship as he sets about doing his duties as a pastor. Note – the minister is not to spend all his time with church members; he is also called to be an evangelist to those who have not heard the good news of the gospel (v. 5).

Discharging the duties of ministry can become a burden, and the responsibility to preach can weigh you down. Ministering to people can be wearisome and I guarantee this, Steve, you will face discouragements. I freely confess there have been times in my life when I have said to the Lord, 'I don't want to be a pastor and I would rather be a bus driver or preferably a jazz pianist.' I confess these two occupations were my childhood ambitions!

When you fail as a pastor, you freely confess your failures to the church family and seek God's cleansing and renewing power. There will be seasons in your ministry when the spiritual fire in your life is burning low and it is in these moments you need to guard your character. Reflecting on my years of ministry, I regret I did not pray more earnestly for the members of the congregation, especially naming those who I knew found it difficult to accept me as their pastor. I should have prayerfully prepared myself in advance, asking the Lord to help me to 'keep [my] head in all situations' – and endure the suffering that comes when people antagonise you and misinterpret your motives.

The great thing about being part of a marvellous church family like Upton Vale is that they are there to support you when you fail, and when the fire burns low, they know when to throw logs of encouragements on your fire.

Years ago, I remember receiving a letter from a church member following a very difficult church meeting. It was the kind of church meeting where afterwards I had despaired and said, 'I don't want to be a pastor, I would rather be a bus driver, but preferably a jazz pianist!' The letter from this church member was like logs on the fire that had burned very low. Her kind words reminded me that I was a good pastor:

I had visited her mother when she was in the hospice.
I had preached at her uncle's funeral.
I had baptised her son before he went to university.

The biggest logs on the minister's fire often come from the prayers and encouragements of church members. The whole congregation helps the ministry team to guard their characters, and the greatest encouragement of all is to know the fire can never go out. It cannot be extinguished because the fire has been lit by the Holy Spirit.

5. Finish well (vv. 6-8)

A bishop was visiting a local parish church as the guest preacher and when he finished his sermon, the congregation clapped him. As he sat down, he remarked to the vicar that never previously had one of his sermons been applauded. The vicar replied courageously, 'I think they are clapping, Bishop, because you've finished!'

It may seem strange on an induction day to speak of finishing well, but this is the advice the older pastor gives to the younger minister. This is the final duty. Paul is nearing the end of his ministry and offers his own experience as an encouragement. Throughout his ministry Paul had presented his body as 'a living sacrifice' (Romans 12:1) in God's service.

As he reaches the end of ministry, he says to Timothy that he feels his life is 'poured out like a drink offering' (v. 6). The Old Testament describes various animal sacrifices

(Numbers 15) where the final part of the animal sacrifice was accompanied by the pouring on the altar of a litre of wine. Paul uses this sacrifice imagery to describe how he was finishing his ministry. He felt his life was ebbing away like a bottle of wine being drained to the dregs. He then adds the image of a ship setting sail, as he expresses the time has come for his departure (v. 6). He pictures a ship casting off its mooring ropes, weighing anchor and departing the harbour for a distant shore.

Looking back over the years of his ministry, Paul professes to have run a good race and fought a good fight, and above all he had 'kept the faith' (v. 7). All three phrases convey what it means to finish well. I like the image of an athletics contest where an athlete has given everything, in order to win. Think of Andy Murray collapsing on Centre Court, Wimbledon in 2013, after his gruelling five sets to defeat Djokovic to win the Men's Singles final. Remember Ben Stokes, in 2019, collapsing to his knees with exhaustion after his match winning innings of eighty-four to win England the Cricket World Cup at Lord's Cricket Ground.

Finish well by presenting your life as a living sacrifice.
Finish well by giving it everything you've got.
Finish well by seeing the reward that awaits those who discharge the duties of their ministry.

The reward to those who finish well is not a cup or a medal but a crown (v. 8). A laurel crown was worn on the head by athletes who had won the race – it is the equivalent of the Olympic gold medal awarded today. This reward of a crown is not just for faithful ministers; it is the crown of righteousness that God awards to all his faithful disciples.

We are all called to run the same race with the same level of perseverance – with a view to receiving the same award!

One of my Christian heroes is John Stott, one of the greatest preachers of the twentieth century. He was God's gift to busy pastors with his lucid Bible commentaries – and thousands of people were blessed by his preaching and his writings. He died at the age of ninety in 2011 and his memorial service was held in St Paul's Cathedral. His final public address was at the Keswick Convention in 2007 when he shared these words on finishing well:

I want to share with you where my mind has come to rest as I approach the end of my pilgrimage on earth - and it is – God wants his people to become like Christ. Christlikeness is the will of God for the people of God.[48]

---

48. John Stott, *The Last Word: Reflections on a Lifetime of Preaching* (Milton Keynes: Authentic, 2008).

Sam Ridgway is my grandson and he and Katie Brown were married on 8 August 2022 at St Aldate's Church, Oxford. I was honoured to give this wedding sermon from the Bible passage they had chosen.

Sam wrote to me a month before the wedding because he knew I was preparing for the great day.

He said, 'Katie and I have been chatting about the service and we want to be as Jesus-focused as possible. It is really not about us, but about what makes us, us (i.e. Jesus) if that makes sense and the Colossians passage is great for this.'

They were particularly concerned about their friends who would be at the service who did not share their Christian faith and hoped I would take this into account in preparing.

13

Lifestyle For a Christian Marriage

Colossians 3:12-15

Thank you for your thoughtful preparations for your wedding day and your attention to the fine details. This includes providing me with the Bible passage to speak from, and you have provided two possible timings for my sermon.

Katie, you suggested a fixed time appropriate to a wedding service. Sam, you were your usual laid-back self and said, 'Take as long as you like, Grandad.'

To everyone's relief, I will be following Katie's advice!

I want to speak to you as a married couple and invite your family and friends to listen in.

I know that, as followers of Jesus, you are not a religious couple. This is because you are relational in your Christian faith – and relational is more personal than being religious.

You know *who* you are because you know *whose* you are. You have a personal relationship with Jesus Christ and are wholly devoted to him. This personal relationship is seen in two ways.

In the first place, your lifestyle as a married couple will be shaped by your love for God. Your desire is to put him first and please him in everything. You are planning a Christ-centred marriage, and in the words of the passage you chose, you intend to 'set your minds on [Christ]' and do everything 'in word and deed . . . in the name of the Lord Jesus' (Colossians 3:2;17).

The second way your faith is personal, is that you have received, as a free gift, the life of Christ into your lives which means there are three of you in this marriage. In fact, the light of Jesus in your hearts is none other than the God who first said on the morning of creation: 'Let there be light [in the darkness]' (Genesis 1:3). God who, by his mighty power, raised Jesus from the grave, shares his power in your lives.

This life of God in you is never picked up on a CT scan because your life with Christ is 'hidden with Christ in God' (Colossians 3:3). But you know it's real and personal.

You choose to nurture this inward spiritual life:

By sharing your faith with each other and with other believers.
By talking to God in prayer.
By reading the Bible.
And of course, by living the Christian life in the world of work.

The Bible is a unique book. It's God's book and he speaks to us through its words. Its writings are thousands of years old, but as we read the Bible, God builds a bridge of understanding between the ancient words and the modern world. You have chosen as your Bible reading a letter written to a group of Christians 2,000 years ago. They lived in a city called Colossae, which is why the book is called Colossians.

The passage you have selected from Colossians 3:12-15, which describes the lifestyle for a Christian, but I want to suggest it is comprehensive lifestyle for a Christian marriage.

What a gathering you have today of family and friends. We are experiencing the combined talents and gifts of the Brown and Ridgway families! Later we will see dozens of photos on display featuring your childhood days and this will generate discussions of family likeness. People will observe: 'Katie – you are so like this relative, and Sam – you are the image of that relative.' As followers of Jesus, the fundamental likeness determining your character and personality is not your likeness to a family member, it is your likeness to Jesus Christ. This all begins with the word *'chosen'*. 'Therefore, as God's *chosen* people' (v. 12, my italics).

This is a day when we celebrate choices. When you first met here at St Aldate's, Sam thought Katie was way out of his league and Katie thought Sam was incredibly good-looking. She had the sun in her eyes at the time!

But we all agree – in choosing each other you have made a great choice. Choosing to be follower of Jesus is of a different order. You have been chosen by God and it's his initiative. You didn't choose to follow Jesus. He took the initiative to choose you and shape your lives. That's why he calls you 'holy and dearly loved' (v. 12). Holy doesn't mean perfect; it implies God loves you so much that he has set you apart as a married couple for his purposes.

You were chosen by God when you were single, and your lives had great significance as single people. But God saw a greater potential in you as a married couple, and you have no idea how your lifelong commitment to each other will bring blessings to many people. Remember you are entering your marriage with flaws, but in partnership with

Christ there will be deep character changes in both of you through your deep friendship.

Don't look for perfection in each other, rather consider yourselves a work in progress. From today there is a work to be done and for this to happen you have to be 'well dressed'! The verse here says 'as God's chosen people . . . *clothe yourselves*' (v. 12, my italics).

Clothing is an appropriate word for your wedding day. Once your wedding invitation was sent to your guests a few months ago, it ignited dozens of conversations on what clothes would be worn. Don't look round now, but I can assure you all your guests are very well turned-out today, and you two look perfect! But as you know the invitation to 'clothe yourselves' is not referring to wedding-day clothes; it is referring to clothes of character, specifically five virtues of character. Why these five virtues? Because they were seen in the life of Jesus, and God wants to reproduce them in your lives. He wants you to reflect the family likeness so that you become gradually more like Jesus. When you become a follower of Christ, you are presented with a new wardrobe of clothes and the old wardrobe needs to be ditched. This old set of clothes is vividly described in verses 5-10. Your calling is to start wearing the new clothes God provides, and this is a process of putting off the old and putting on the new.

I sent you list of questions a few weeks ago and asked you not to share your answers with each other. It was a form of Mr and Mrs Quiz before your wedding day and I can now reveal some the results! I asked for your top items from your long-term bucket list and Katie replied that top of her list was: 'Having a home that we can use for hosting and welcoming people, so that everyone feels able to drop by, and there's always time and food for people.' Sam – you said your top three items were:

'Owning a Bernese Mountain Dog.
Visiting Yosemite National Park.
And meeting Bob Mortimer.'

Here is another revelation from the quiz answers. I asked Sam if Katie had ever said, 'Please don't play rugby Sam, as it will spoil your good looks.' Sam, you replied, 'Yes, Katie has said that many times.' But when I asked Katie whether she had any objections to Sam playing rugby, she replied, 'Absolutely not! I'd love to see him play more, and maybe Sam will play for a team again one day!' Now I share these intimate quiz results not to cast a shadow over this perfect day, but to remind you there is work to be done of getting to know each other and harmonising your life together.

The basis of a good marriage begins with being clothed with these five virtues – 'compassion, kindness, humility, gentleness and patience' (v. 12).

Here is the first virtue:

1. Be clothed with compassion

In the old language of the Bible, compassion is called 'Bowels of mercy', indicating there is something physiological about compassion. It lies deep within a person which is why, positively, we refer to someone having heartfelt compassion, or negatively we comment that their heart just wasn't in it. Compassion is being moved to the very core of your being. The Latin root for the word 'passion' means to suffer, so that *com*-passion means suffering *with* another person.

Some things you are hearing today won't make sense, but one day in your marriage you will be drawing on the rich resource of compassion to see you through a challenging time.

2. Be clothed with kindness

In the Mr and Mrs Quiz, when I asked you what qualities you admired in each other, both of you used the word 'kindness'. Katie, you said of Sam: 'I love his generosity and kindness with others, and the welcome he always gives people no matter who they are.' Sam, you said of Katie: 'I admire her endless kindness and gentleness. She has the ability to automatically look for the best in people rather than criticise faults or failings.'

It's great to observe that you are both already wearing the clothing of kindness.

3. Be clothed with humility

Your understanding of humility will always be shaped by the example of Christ, the mighty ruler of the universe who became a speechless baby in the Bethlehem manger. Be like Christ and think humbly and live humbly.

You are an exceptionally gifted couple, but you know that all the good gifts you possess come from your generous heavenly Father. Gratitude should accompany humility. I suggest you touch the wall of your new home and say: 'Thank you, Lord.' When reviewing your online bank accounts, remember to say: 'Thank you, Lord.' The humble Christian couple look at everything and say with gratitude, 'Lord, this is all yours and we are grateful.'

4. Be clothed with gentleness

You need this virtue for your life together in the home, but also, in your worlds of business and education. Gentleness is the most countercultural of Christian virtues. In an aggressive, competitive and often angry culture, where you are encouraged to fight and struggle in order to find your place in the sun – gentleness refuses to be consumed by what others are doing.

Instead, you will trust in the Lord who himself is 'gentle and humble in heart' (Matthew 11:29) and allow him to direct your destiny.

5. Be clothed with patience

This is a very important virtue in marriage. It's the long fuse, not the short temper.

As Grandma Janet will share, you will need an endless supply of this virtue. She is often heard saying to me, 'I'm running out of my patience.' As you've probably observed, it is simple things that can trigger conflict in the home.

This practical virtue of patience turns away from revenge and reprisals, and instead it demonstrates a willingness to endure imperfections. You 'bear with each other' and forgive grievances. Your standard is the pattern set forth by Jesus; you are to forgive each other 'as the Lord forgave you' (v. 13).

You know the well-known saying about the twelve most important words in a marriage?

It has been suggested they are:

I was wrong.
I am sorry.

Please forgive me.
I love you.

Having shared the five virtues, the finishing flourish is in verse 14: 'And over all these virtues put on love, which binds everything together in perfect unity.'

1 Corinthians 13 is a Bible passage often read at weddings and begins with the reminder that wearing these five virtues of character can contribute to some amazing achievements. You can have faith to move mountains; you can give all your money to the poor; you can even go to the stake and be burned as a martyr for the faith . . . which is all impressively virtuous, but without love – they count for nothing. True love is patient, kind and never gives up; it is never boastful arrogant or rude; it always protects and perseveres. This is the quality of love which will never fail you. It's the topcoat which completes the wedding outfit! It holds everything together and enables you to survive the stress tests of marriage.

You have already acknowledged these stresses in your wedding vows:

Sickness or health
Better or worse
Richer or poorer

To face these stress tests, over everything put on love.

You don't drift into this marriage lifestyle. First – it's a choice; second – it's a lifelong labour of love, and third – you will need to depend daily on God's enabling power. He alone provides the power to love that you don't possess. Your natural supply to love each other will dry up, but God's resources will provide you with an endless supply.

Your wedding day is a public occasion and we have been invited to attend and witness that Sam and Katie declare from today they are husband and wife. From now on you are Mr and Mrs Ridgway. Just as your wedding day is public, so your marriage will be on view.

Your relationship will be like a book that can be read and a drama that can be viewed, but please don't be daunted by that prospect. All you have to do is learn the lines of the parts you are called to play as husband and wife, with Christ as the head of your home.

Older guests will recall the BBC television show *Parkinson*. It was a popular Saturday night programme which featured Michael Parkinson interviewing various guests, film stars, actors and sports personalities. One evening Michael Parkinson was interviewing Michael Caine, the actor. Parkinson asked him: 'What's the difference between a movie star and a movie actor?'

Michael Caine replied, 'The movie star says: "how can I change the script of the story to suit my personality?" The great movie actor says: "how can I change myself to fit the script and the story line?"'[49]

In the drama of marriage, you are like two great actors.

If you both say today, 'How can we change ourselves to fit God's script for marriage?'

Then I guarantee – that will be a box office hit!

---

49. Philip Greenslade, *A Passion for God's Story: Discovering Your Place in God's Strategic Plan* (Milton Keynes: Paternoster Press, 2002), p. 242.

Addresses

The National Baptist Leaders' Day was held on 13 March 1999 at the Wembley Conference Centre, London.

Two thousand six hundred local church leaders gathered from across the United Kingdom to explore what shape the Baptist Union of GB would be in the new millennium.

Following the Denominational Consultation in September 1996, several reforms were proposed which were designed to renew the life of the Baptist Union and its structures.

Many local church leaders had not been part of the reform process and the Wembley Leaders' Day was designed to inform a wider group of Baptists what changes were being proposed and inspire them with a fresh vision of being Baptists together.

This was the keynote address at the conclusion of the day.

14

National Baptist Leaders' Day
Wembley 1999

Isaiah 35

Thank you for coming to this National Leaders' Day. Someone said to me in the last few days they would never have thought so many people would be willing to book a day at Wembley not knowing the details of the event. Well, you did, and I am glad you are here. I can imagine some of you are here today because someone asked you to attend the event and it was easier to say 'yes' than decline the offer. Others would openly say they know very little of the Baptist Union, and this kind of gathering is not their usual scene, but as a leader in a local church they thought they should be present. Some have said to me they are eager for the proposed reforms to be put in place so they can on with the urgent task of mission. Yet others, supporting lowly football clubs, thought this was their best chance of getting to Wembley!

I want to return to the Bible passage with which we began – Isaiah 35. In the previous chapter, Isaiah has described a desert scene which is intended to depict the times in which he lived. When he surveys the political, social, moral and spiritual landscape of his times he uses terms such as thorns and brambles, smouldering buildings and a land drenched with the blood of people. These were dark days of judgement.

By contrast, chapter 35 is the rainbow after the storm. It is the dawn of a new morning of God's grace following the thunder and lightning of his judgement. The verses of chapter 35 pulsate with hope. They brought encouragement to the people for whom they were first written.

They are for our encouragement today. There are some key truths in this chapter that we need to understand as we move towards our moment of commitment in this Leaders' Day.

1. A vision of kingship (Isaiah 6:1-5)

Isaiah believed that God was the true King of the universe and one day the whole world would know it. If the prophet was here this afternoon and we invited him to say a few words of testimony – if we said to him, 'You lived in uncertain times when international influences were driving national politics, when there was moral confusion in the nation, and you were distressed by the spiritual half-heartedness of God's people – speak a word of encouragement to us', Isaiah might respond by saying, 'I suggest you live by the vision God gives you. The direction of my life was determined by what I saw in a worship service. In the year that yet another earthly king had died, I saw *the* King with fresh eyes. I received a vision of God as King of the universe and knew in that moment that he is the Lord, and he reigns on high. I developed this conviction that either God is King who rules supreme, or he is no King at all. His truth has to be proclaimed over the whole of life and from that moment I lived my life by that sustaining vision. I learned never to doubt in the darkness what God had shown me in the light.'

Friends, I would die a happy man if as a result of this exercise of reform we became a Baptist people who fostered a deeper commitment to the Lord; that every baptised believer was able to say with Abraham Kuyper: 'There is not a square inch in the whole domain of human existence over which Christ, who is Sovereign over all, does not cry: "Mine!"';[50] that every church lived by the maxim: 'We cannot preach good news and live in our community as bad news'; that every pastor was true to their calling and was prepared to live heroically for Jesus, so that what God showed to them in private was boldly proclaimed in public; that if the congregation pray for the fire of the Holy Spirit to descend on the preacher, they might expect the minister to burn in the pulpit; that if all Baptists understood they were part of a much bigger plan God had for his world, then our tiny steps of reforms might be seen as a bigger footprint of God's kingdom.

God gave to Isaiah a kingdom-of-God vision that went far beyond his life and time and we need this larger vision today.

What Isaiah prophesied touched the life and times of Jesus, which is why he chose to speak from Isaiah 61 when he commenced his preaching ministry.

---

50. Speech by Abraham Kuyper at the opening of the Free University Amsterdam 1880. The full speech is available on www.gospelcoalition.org (accessed 20.5.23). It is titled 'Sphere Sovereignty'.

It touched the life and times of the early Church, which is why Philip, the hitch-hiking evangelist, found he was starting with Isaiah 53 when leading an African to Christ.

It influenced the apostle John in his visionary book of Revelation. You could subtitle his book *The Empire Strikes Back*. God inspired John to write about the death of death and hell's destruction. He saw that a new day would dawn when tears would be wiped away and God would create a new heaven and new earth, and all this wrapped up in boundless joy.

This language is the very hallmark of Isaiah in chapter 35.

We need this larger vision of the King and the kingdom! We are not today speaking of narrow denominational interests that will advance the Baptist cause. I urge you from the heart to discern that all our discussions, debates and decisions are seen in this context. Let us place everything we possess – documents, reports, dreams and personal ambitions – on the altar of God and say together: 'For the King and his kingdom'!

2. A vision of a transformed desert (35:1-2)

Here is a poetic picture of the desert bursting into flower after heavy rainfall and this brings joy to the world. Flowers shout for joy and nature bursts into song for the good things God has done. We should share in this joy when we see the blossoming of our deserts:

When BMS youth action teams flood our churches with their enthusiasm and concern for global mission. When Baptists in the north-west of England take their puppet theatre into dozens of schools and tell the story of Jesus to hundreds of children.

When Christians in south London go door knocking in an area where 60 per cent of young black men are unemployed and ask the question: 'Have you a young person living here who has been unemployed for six months – because we would like to offer help?'
When during the past ten years, £22 million has generously been given by people like you in support of Baptist Home Mission in the United Kingdom.
When a church of twenty members baptises one new disciple.

These are all symbols of fruitfulness in desolate places, and we should rejoice in the flowering of the desert places, but we should be crying out to God for those desert places which have yet to be transformed.

One of the most challenging pieces of writing last year came from the journalist Nick Davies who visited some of the *dark heart* areas of Britain and described in stark detail what he found:[51]

Children caught up in the sex trade;
Families ravaged by crack cocaine;
The juvenile thief;
The teenage prostitute;
Young men, jobless without hope, propping up a wall in the morning – sleeping during the afternoon – watching the telly till dawn.

It's a desert place when there are needy neighbourhoods in our society:

---

51. Nick Davies, *Dark Heart: The Shocking Truth about Hidden Britain* (NY: Vintage, 1998).

When children go to school hungry;
When 1 million children play truant each year;
When 1,300 children are permanently excluded from school;
When teenagers grow up with no job prospects.

It's a desert place when we are blind to the have-nots in our own Baptist family. We have churches in membership with our Union where no one apart from the minister is a regular wage earner. There was a cartoon depicting a boat in a rough sea and the boat was obviously damaged and sinking fast. There was a group of people standing at the end of boat which was still out of the water and saying to each other, 'We are so glad that we chose to sit this end of the boat.'

We need to reverse the self-centred culture which looks after the narrow self-interests of *my* church and *our* fellowship. A Union renewed in its relationships knows the meaning of the word *'others'*.

It's desert place when 3 billion people worldwide live on less than £1.50 per day. That is why, for all the encouragements concerning our own government's continuing commitment to the values of Jubilee 2000, we need to keep the pressure up to cut the debt and boost the funding of overseas aid.

It's a desert place when the killers of Stephen Lawrence are still walking free. And it's a barren desert place when Baptists fail to name the racism of their heart. That pernicious racism which sees ethnic background as a problem in society instead of a rainbow gift of diversity from heaven.

And what of the desert place of spiritual ignorance and unbelief? We should weep for the famine of a basic knowledge of the gospel story and pray for the restoration of the forgotten language of God's love for the lost revealed in Jesus Christ.

An earlier generation knew and lived by this language of seeking and saving the lost. They understood evangelism was the lifeline for a believer's church tradition. You evangelise or you cease to exist.

3. A vision of encouragement in a waiting period (35:3-4)

Every vision from God has to wait its moment of birth. I was thinking about those visions we saw on the screen at the beginning of the afternoon. From Martin Luther King and the USA to Mo Mowlam and Northern Ireland, it was a reminder that all visions appear to have built-in impossibilities. We need to look at what has been accomplished in the last decade. It was boldly declared of the seemingly impossible:

Apartheid will never end!
The Berlin Wall will stand for ever!
Peace settlement in Northern Ireland is impossible!

Scripture is full of this principle of the seemingly impossible. When Mary heard that she would bear the child Jesus and declared she found it a mystery how a virgin could conceive and bear a child, God's response was: 'Nothing [is] impossible with God' (Luke 1:37, ESV). The Lord has his way of caring for his visions. He has his timing for bringing those visions to birth and what we need in a waiting period is the encouragement to be strong and steady, waiting patiently for the vision to come to birth – which is where we are right now as a Baptist people.

The prophet highlights three critical areas of weakness in the waiting period. He mentions their hands, their knees and their hearts. Described by the prophet as 'feeble hands', unsteady knees and 'fearful hearts'. Why are these crucial parts of the spiritual anatomy?

Because when we see a vision, our hands are raring to go. But until the vision becomes reality, what is there to do with our hands? There is the temptation to feel useless and think the vision will never happen.

God says: 'Strengthen those feeble hands!'

When you are standing around waiting for things to happen, it is tempting to lose heart and walk away; to sit down and relax or turn away and do something else.

God says: 'Stand firm on your unsteady knees and wait!'

The most dangerous part of the spiritual body is the fearful heart. Fear can become impetuous. It can panic and make the wrong choices. The fearful heart pulls back from the brink and has forgotten that sometimes we have to die to our personal visions in order to gain God's way of doing things. The fearful heart needs to hear the promise when God says, 'I will come to save you' (v.4).

Imagine the tombstone epitaphs which might be written for this generation of Baptists: They enjoyed great fellowship and worship. They were faithful in their duties, but they lost the vision God gave them and they died clinging to things which were unimportant.

Might it be said of us:

They made the necessary sacrifices.
They discovered new ways of being the Church.
They were obedient to the heavenly vision.

4. A vision of salvation (35:5-7)

Salvation means rescuing those who are helpless. The people in these verses are described as blind, deaf, lame and dumb. This speaks of the absolute helplessness of the human condition unless God steps in to save and rescue. The appropriate response to helplessness is always to cry to God for rescue. In the late eighteenth century it was the custom of pastors in the Northamptonshire Baptist Association to meet periodically for prayer and fasting. These were ministers clustering together, relating and resourcing each other, concerned for the renewal of the Church and its mission to the whole world. Their chief design was to implore the Lord to send a spiritual revival in their souls, in their churches, and in the land at large.

Believers only pray like this when they see the spiritual helplessness of their condition. Remember the way of Jesus with people as a reminder of his way with us today:

See yourself as blind Bartimaeus and cry out: 'Lord, I want to see!'
See yourself as the lame man at the Temple and cry out: 'Lord, I want to walk!'
See your church as a dead Lazarus lying in the tomb.
Hear the voice of the risen Lord at the door of the church saying:
'Awake sleepers from the dead, and live!'

Many times, I have said over these reforms what I have said over a local church of which I was pastor: 'Lord, this situation needs your touch of power.'

We need to be asking the Lord in his mercy to come and save us:

By your mighty power transform us.
Open our eyes to see you at work in our midst.
Open our ears to hear your voice guiding us.
Open our mouths so that we can say 'yes' to your commands.
Give us strength to walk once again in your paths.
Come in your power and transform our desert landscape (vv. 6-7)
Grant us one flower – one oasis – a small stream.
Let the burning sand become a pool of water.
Send us something to assure our weak hearts.

5. A vision of a road (35:8-10)

And suddenly a road appears in the desert. What previously has been a desert landscape with no traceable path, a trackless waste of endless sand dunes, suddenly in the vision there appears the gift of a road. It is called a highway of holiness. The road was travelled by Ezra and Nehemiah on their return from exile. John the Baptist powered his way down this road shouting: 'Fill in the potholes and remove the rocks and boulders. Here comes the King!'

Jesus travelled this road on his way into Jerusalem.

The disciples, after his death and resurrection and the gift of the Holy Spirit, took this road out of Jerusalem, and with God's power and direction they commenced building a network of gospel highways which now stretch to all parts of the globe. And our lesser road is somehow linked to this greater highway.

All we have heard today concerns a new journey God is calling us to make together. It is a road that has to be walked. If we do not walk this road, then our visions are never born in flesh and blood. It's a road for the committed and the moment of commitment has come. This is an important moment in our lives as a Baptist people. Perhaps an important moment in your life.

It is just possible that God would use a day designed for one purpose to be a blessing for a greater purpose.

My mind goes back to June 1984 when I was attending the opening meeting of Mission England. Billy Graham was the preacher at Ashton Gate Stadium, Bristol. It was a Saturday afternoon, and I could ill afford the time away from my study with two Sunday services fast approaching. I had travelled with a coach party which included people who did not know Jesus. I confess I was there on duty as a pastor. If I hadn't been present in Bristol, questions would have been asked!

But God spoke to me as a disciple of Jesus through that event and I believe it changed my preaching ministry from that day forwards. As I sat high in the stands of the stadium listening to the preaching of Billy Graham and then watched as hundreds responded to the gospel appeal, I was strangely moved in my spirit and heard the Lord saying to me, 'I need you as participant in my mission, not as a spectator.' I consider that Saturday afternoon a turning point in my ministry. It is sometimes good for pastors and leaders to make a fresh commitment.

This is God's appeal to our hearts *this* Saturday afternoon. Will you love Jesus Christ so much that you will freshly commit yourself to him and play your part in these reforms as the Lord directs you?

Moment of induction with the family

The celebration of 100 years of ministry of the Baptist World Alliance (BWA) was a historic event. It took place at the Birmingham National Indoor Arena on Saturday, 30 July 2005.

The BWA had been founded in London in 1905 when 80 per cent of the global Christian population was in Europe and North America.

In 2005, 60 per cent of the world's Christians were found in Africa, Asia and Latin America and 50 per cent of the 12,000 attending were from these continents.

As a sign of the times, 2,000 from Africa, Asia and Latin America were refused visas to attend.

It was an honour to be inducted into my five years of international ministry in my home country, a privilege not always afforded to an incoming BWA president.

15

Acceptance Speech as President of the Baptist World Alliance 2005

I stand here today with a great sense of gratitude to you all, and an even greater sense of the tremendous privilege that you have entrusted to me in calling me to serve as your president.

To experience the love and trust of the global family is overwhelming, and I now seek the anointing of the Holy Spirit for the ministry that awaits me. As I look now to the next five years, I want briefly to share with you the values that will shape my presidency.

First, *I believe in the gospel.* For the Bible says it is 'the power of God' for salvation for 'everyone who believes' (Romans 1:16). I affirm my commitment to be a Great Commission Christian and stand firmly in that tradition that says, 'every Baptist a missionary'. Too often the world is more aware of what the Church is against than what it is for; and this is no strategy for winning lost people to Jesus Christ. We need to be more like Jesus – to earn the reputation of being friends to sinners and to give ourselves in sacrificial service for a broken world.

Second, *I believe in the Church*, and in the paramount importance of the unity of the Church. Jesus prayed that we would be one, that the world may believe (John 17:21). Unity is a gospel imperative, and disunity is always a major hindrance to evangelism. The urgent question in all our churches is: 'How do we live with our deepest differences?' God's sign to a disunited world is the Church, united in Jesus Christ. I also believe in a future for the Church and our responsibility as the Baptist World Alliance to raise up a new generation of emerging leaders who will serve as international ambassadors for Christ.

Thirdly, *I believe in worship.* Worship that is connected to the real world. Worship which breeds a discontent with the way the world is, and which enables us to see the world as God sees it. Remember, 'To clasp the hands in prayer are the beginning of an uprising against the disorder of the world.'[52] Which is why justice and compassion are the hallmarks of true worship. I affirm the Micah Challenge – 'to act justly, love mercy and walk humbly with my God' (see Micah 6:8).

To make poverty history is the duty of every Christian and we should not need the world to tell us so. It is an acid test of our obedience to follow Jesus when he says: 'inasmuch as you did it to . . . the least of these . . . you did it to Me' (Matthew 25:40, NKJV). We cannot strive to be more like Jesus if we have a lifestyle less like Jesus. I will gladly support the BWA as it continues to be a voice for the voiceless. There are 250 million Christians who are persecuted for their faith, and in the words of Scripture – we need to speak up for those who can't speak for

---

52. Karl Barth (1886-1968), www.goodreads.com/quotes/1601-to-clasp-the-hands-in-prayer-is-the-beginning-of (accessed 25.4.23).

themselves (Proverbs 31:9). This means challenging those authorities who exercise might without morality and power without compassion.

Many of you have stopped me over the past few days to share your growing sense that God is preparing a new thing among us. These are days of great challenge for the people of God in a fearful and uncertain world. And in a world without hope, we must be the people who see the rainbow of God's promises, though the storm clouds are gathered round. Some of our greatest moments as Baptists have arisen during trial and adversity. Although this morning, in a formal sense, is a time of dedication for me as your president, it can be so much more, it must be so much more. I challenge you in this moment to join me in making a renewed commitment to Jesus Christ and his service; to answer the call given by our outgoing president, Dr Billy Kim, and say to the Lord, 'Here am I. Send me' (Isaiah 6:8). May God grant us all the grace we need to live for him alone.

Aim4Excellence was a conference held at Swanwick Conference Centre in October 2007.

It was planned by senior managers from Anthony Collins Solicitors, the Evangelical Alliance, Global Connections, Spring Harvest and Stewardship.

It was attended by executives from more than 200 Christian charities and aimed to provide practical input and advice on best practice as well as spiritual refreshment and a unique environment for networking.

I was invited to give this opening address, and it is an abbreviated version.

16

The Seven Distinctives of the Christian Organisation

I congratulate those who had the vision to organise this very timely conference. Firstly, it offers a huge potential for networking with others who possess kingdom resources, and I hope that a major outcome of *Aim4Excellence* will be some imaginative partnerships.

Secondly, it fosters evangelical unity. In my lifetime, evangelical unity has been never so threatened. There are moments when I feel we are losing the ground that we gained in the 1970s and 1980s when we honoured and accepted one another across the denominational and organisational divisions. It grieves my spirit that we cannot find a greater gospel unity when we are facing such a great missionary opportunity in the UK and we have the epic Micah Challenge[53] to make poverty history, in partnership with the world Church.

The third reason I am grateful for this conference, is to praise the high standards of professional excellence

---

53. www.micahchallenge.org.uk/ (accessed 24.4.23).

which I observe in numerous Christian charities, and we are here to share these good practices. But this conference is equally an opportunity to remember the warning of Francis Schaeffer: 'The real problem is this: the church of the Lord Jesus Christ, individually or corporately, tending to do the Lord's work in the power of the flesh rather than of the Spirit. The central problem is always in the midst of the people of God, not in the circumstances surrounding them.'[54]

You have invited me to address in this opening session the question: 'What is distinctive about a Christian charity? What difference does it make that we are a Christian body? What are the practical steps we can take to assure we not just Christian in name?'

Christians in a secular workplace may find principles in what I share, but I propose seven unique distinctives for the Christian organisation.

1. The first Christian distinctive is having a basic theology for the workplace

This theology is the creation partnership we enjoy with God. From the opening pages of the Bible, God is represented as a worker. Day by day his creative plan unfolded and when God finished his work, he pronounced it as good. God experienced job satisfaction. God's final act of creation is the creation of human beings and as a gift he made us workers too. We are called into this partnership of ruling, filling and subduing the earth (Genesis 1:28-30).

First, we are given our worth as human beings – we are made in God's image. Then we are given our work as co-

---

54. Francis Schaeffer, *No Little People* (Wheaton, IL: Crossway, 2003), p. 66.

workers with God in his amazingly complex and beautiful universe. God is the worker and because we are made in his image, all our work finds its meaning in him.

This partnership with God-the-worker is built into our very beings. It is so central a focus that if we do not take seriously our daily work as service to the Lord, then we are defying the very purpose for which we have been created. Our daily work is an expression of this partnership with God.

There is a management responsibility which emerges from the Genesis command to 'rule, fill and subdue'. This work can be done sinfully with no reference to God, as with the builders of the Tower of Babel (Genesis 11) or we can do it obediently, following God's leadership, as with the marine architect Noah (Genesis 6-9). We are the original *friends of the earth* who can never misread God's command to 'rule, fill and subdue', as 'rape, plunder and destroy'.

Howard Snyder is professor of history and theology at Asbury Theological Seminary, Kentucky. He says the environment should be demonstration plots for our concern for God's world. He also suggests that a commitment to recycling is an echo of a kingdom patriotism:

If patriotic Christians during World War II could recycle tin cans and tires for the war effort, certainly Jesus' disciples today can recycle our abundance of consumer trash, demonstrating kingdom patriotism.[55]

The fall was a catastrophe for humankind, and what should have been a joyous working partnership with God

---

55. Howard Snyder, 'Why We Love the Earth', *Christianity Today*, 15 May 1995, www.christianitytoday.com/ct/1995/may15/5t6015.html (accessed 25.4.23).

has become a futile enterprise. When this concept of a management partnership with God disappears, then work *can* become a sweat to stay alive (Genesis 3:19).

This burden of work is well captured by Ecclesiastes:

> So I hated life, because the work that is done under the sun was grievous to me. . . . I hated all the things I had toiled for under the sun, because I must leave them to the one who comes after me. . . . [What does a worker get for all his work?] All his days his work is pain and grief; even at night his mind does not rest. This too is meaningless.
>
> *(Ecclesiastes 2:17-23, NIV 1984)*

For the believer, there should never be futility in the workplace. Staff members who are new Christians or staff who have been poorly discipled may not realise this Christian distinctive. When we confess Jesus as Lord and Saviour this is worked out in the context of home, church *and* the workplace. Whatever we do, by word of deed we 'do it all in the name of the Lord Jesus' (Colossians 3:17). We do our job to the Lord not to people (Colossians 3:23) for 'it is the Lord Christ [we] are serving' (Colossians 3:25).

Jesus is ever present among us to teach his apprentices how to do the best and aim for excellence. It may seem like the ABC of the Christian workplace, but I would want to make sure that every staff member in a Christian organisation is able to confess that God is working in this place, and I am working with him.

2. The second distinctive for the Christian organisation is making the workplace the primary place of discipleship.

This implies there will be a spirituality of discipleship which is consciously fostered by the Christian organisation. I like the emphasis of Dallas Willard, that to be a disciple you are willing to be mentored by Jesus so that you do your work as he would have it done.[56]

If we don't think like this, then we are choosing to run one of the largest areas of our life under the instruction of people other than Jesus. So how do we make the Christian organisation the primary place of discipleship?

First of all, we guarantee that each believer has a Christian understanding of their personal identity in Christ. We teach that, because of Jesus Christ, we have a worth before we have a work. This is countercultural to the worldly way in which people identify themselves by their work – their job titles, their salary band. We are given an identify as believers through the love of God who made us and saved us.

Secondly, God is working within us, as the master craftsman, shaping us into the image of his Son, Jesus Christ. We must develop, in the mind of the believer, the spiritual sensitivity that God is always at work in our workplace. God is willing and working in us according to his 'good purpose' (Philippians 2:13); God has begun a 'good work' and will complete it (Philippians 1:6); God has created us in Christ Jesus 'to do good works' (Ephesians 2:10).

Thirdly, we need to develop a deeper confidence in Jesus as our mentor for the workplace. We trust him as

---

56. Dallas Willard, 'Renewed for Mission', www.dwillard.org (accessed 10.5.23).

our teacher in matters regarding temptation, prayer and guidance, but what about taking advice for our work from Jesus the worker?

Last week, I was in Nazareth for the opening of the Nazareth Centre for Christian Studies and, during my time there, visited the Nazareth village. This centre has reconstructed a first-century village as Nazareth would have been when Jesus was brought up by Mary and Joseph – and worked in his father's carpenter's shop. I realised afresh that the teaching of Jesus is immersed in the life and problems of working people. His knowledge of the business world of fishing, farming and winegrowing forms the background for much of his teaching on discipleship.

He uses a *security tower in a vineyard* – and suggests that no sensible wine grower would fail to budget for building a tower to guard the crop of vines. This becomes a teaching moment for disciples. If you are not willing to budget for the cost of cross-bearing, you can't be one of my disciples (Luke 14:25-30).

He mentions a *plough* and reminds us that no professional farmer would ever look back when ploughing his field. This is the teaching moment to remind disciples of the need to be single-minded in following Jesus. They need the mindset: 'Nothing and no one is going to distract me from being a disciple. I have started and I intend to finish' (see Luke 9:57-62).

He takes a *fishing boat* and steps into the frenetic teamwork of landing a catch of fish. He then uses this everyday scene of the fishing industry to call the first disciples to the fishing expedition of their lives. He says that the new calling will be to catch people, not fish. For this mission work these experienced fishermen will need divine help. Their human experience and observation alone will not suffice (Luke 5:1-11).

He uses *a wineskin* – which every family would have hanging somewhere in the kitchen area of their home. The basic principle would be understood by the youngest members of the family. If you want to preserve the newly fermented wine, then never use an old wineskin. If you do, the inflexible wineskin will burst and you will lose the new wine. This provides a teaching moment that illustrates the need for flexible structures for the new wine of the kingdom (Luke 5:36-38).

He takes *a mustard seed*, which is tiny and insignificant, and which does a secret, hidden work in the soil. Jesus likens this tiny seed to the dynamic growth of the kingdom of God. We are left asking the question: Who would ever guess that fruitful ministries could emerge form insignificant beginnings (Luke 13:18-19)?

Friends, we need a greater confidence to be taught by Jesus the worker! He is the same today as he was yesterday (Hebrews 13:8). He is not limited to farming, fishing and wine-growing. He knows the business world of the twenty-first century and he can take the familiar images we work with every day and make them into teaching moments.

You may feel this discipleship-making is the task of the local church, not the workplace. I am suggesting it is too important to delegate in the hope that somewhere this discipleship formation is happening. Your task is to guarantee, as a Christian organisation, that it is on the agenda, and you may need some new partnerships in place to deliver it in the workplace.

3. The third distinctive is the provision of a caring working environment where people can grow and develop their potential

I recently read the story of the management consultant who advises churches and Christian organisations that if he wants to know the effectiveness of their ministry, he starts by talking to their cleaning staff. That way he discovers what kind of people are leading the organisation.

I thought he would have an interesting conversation if he talked to the cleaning staff of the office where I used to work. A few years ago, I was working late one night when two of the cleaning staff entered my office and asked me, 'David – will you bless our bingo pens?'

I gave them a caring answer which I don't intend to share with you today – but I assure you, I made it into an evangelistic opportunity!

When I began as CEO of a Christian organisation, we decided as a team to have a session with a Christian management consultancy. We faced the challenging task of making some posts in the organisation redundant and wanted advice on how to achieve pastoral excellence in this time of trauma. I still remember the opening session where the consultants told us of their observation of Christian organisations. In the main, Christian organisations don't know how to hire staff; they don't know how to care for staff; they don't know how to fire staff. They told us people will always remember how we handled this process of redundancy, and the wisdom they offered guided the process. I believe that even the most difficult of decisions can be made in the context of a caring environment. How do we provide a unique caring environment?

In the first place, you make a solid commitment to pray together in the workplace. I am not talking about the formal beginning, and ending a committee meeting with Bible reading and prayer. Nor is it simply scheduling for a fixed time of prayer in the weekly diary. It would be interesting to hear in the discussion groups of the value of the daily or weekly prayers in your organisation.

My observation is that many Christian members of staff think formal prayer times are an intrusion into their working day. Beyond the formal times of corporate prayer is the built-in strategy by which we gain a clear perspective on the world and God's commitment to the world. Prayer enables us to read our times through God's eyes and then respond out of passion for the world.

Secondly, we ensure that our staff truly rest from their work. Rest is more than a weekend recovery from work. The gift of work must be accompanied by a Christian understanding of the rhythm of work and rest. This counters the attitude which seeks to escape into a leisure time which is feverishly hard work!

Many people, including Christians, can work so hard in their leisure time that the periods away from the Christian organisation can become as stressful as the workplace. Rest days are not days to recuperate from work. They are intended as days of reflection. In solitude the heart is called primarily not to do something.

I think every staff member with large creative responsibilities should be encouraged to take regular Sabbaths – and occasional sabbatical periods. It is a distinctive mark of the Christian organisation that it cares for the rest periods as well as the work periods.

4. The fourth distinctive is our ministry must be transformational

Mr Joachim is a Sri Lankan living in Canada. He has an odd passion for accumulating world records based on endurance. He has smashed the record for watching television non-stop (sixty-nine hours and forty-eight minutes); he has set the standard for the time balanced on one foot (seventy-six hours and forty minutes), and for travelling up and down an escalator (seven days). When asked why he engaged in seemingly futile activities, he replied that it was to raise awareness of suffering children. However, his friends suspect he has become so obsessed with record-breaking that he has lost sight of his main objective.[57]

When the work of the Christian organisation has become an end in itself, it is time to take stock. During my visit to the Middle East last week, I met the CEO of the Bible Society for Lebanon. He shared with me some of his ministry distinctives. Primarily their ministry is not about quantity output, such as how many Bibles have been distributed. The *real* question is how the ministry is impacting the lives of people. Thinking this way has made his organisation more holistic in distributing Bibles in Palestinian refugee camps. Alongside Bible distribution, they build relationships, distribute food, form a 'back to your home' programme for displaced people and assist refugees in the conflicts following the 2006 war.

This is more than staying on message as an organisation. It is asking some basic questions about the transformational content of our message. Let me risk another reference to my visit to Nazareth. By now you will appreciate my time in Nazareth was very fruitful in preparing for this address!

57. Tim Hames, *The Times*, 26 September 2005.

As I stood in the reconstructed synagogue in the Nazareth village, I reflected on the sermon Jesus preached – and recalled two features of his ministry which transformed the lives of people (Luke 4:16ff).

First, Jesus had a clear focus why the Holy Spirit was upon him. He knew he was anointed to transform people's lives. It was an anointing that would bring good news for the poor, freedom for the captive, sight to the blind and liberty for the oppressed. And Jesus said this good news was for *today* – not yesterday or a vague someday.

This is the clear focus on transformational ministry for every Christian organisation – an understanding as to *why* God has anointed us for his service. What is the anointing for today? Not yesterday or a vague someday. The work of the organisation cannot become an end in itself. Remember, it is possible to get lost in the tasks and lose sight of *the* task.

The second lesson we learn from the Nazareth sermon is what Jesus preached, he practised. Too often we finish reading Luke 4 at verse 30 where the Nazareth congregation tried to kill him. But we need to read on to verse 31 where Luke wants us to see the transforming ministry of Jesus in Capernaum where there *is* spiritual faith and obedience. At the end of Luke 4 we see the transformational ministry at work with healings in the Capernaum synagogue. Simon's mother-in-law is prayed over and restored to her ministry of hospitality; a demon-possessed man is liberated from his prison house of torment; the people of the community beg Jesus to stay and continue his transforming ministry (Luke 4:31-44).

I want to emphasise at the beginning of this conference that aiming for excellence is not only about visionary statements; quantity and quality of output; efficient programmes and balanced budgets; legally correct trusteeships; professional and trustworthy communication systems. These are vitally important ingredients, but pre-eminently, we are called to change lives and transform communities.

Transformational leadership is the Jesus way of ministry. I believe this is the single most important leadership contribution that the CEO makes to the organisation. Leaders live the dream. They mentor as they model the vision. Their spiritual energy ensures the organisation is not absorbed by the tasks but maintains its focus on *the* task.

5. The fifth distinctive of the Christian organisation is a persistent endeavour to see the core values of the organisation working in action

A few years ago, there was huge multi-national company in the USA which spent millions of dollars taking their staff away to learn their new values. It is a *Harvard Business Review* case study. They developed a new values statement designed to imbue the company's new values into the life of the staff. The four core values were – communication, respect, integrity and excellence. You know the name of the company? Enron.[58]

This fifth distinctive deals with the slippage between words and actions. We all know that a rotten corporate culture produces rotten deeds. The warning to Christian organisations is plain. The most finely crafted statement of core values will not defend you when the hurricanes arrive

---

58. Enron was an American energy company based in Houston, Texas. In 2001 it was revealed the company had been sustained by a systematic and creatively planned accounting fraud. 'The Fall Of Enron', www.hbr.org (accessed 10.5.23).

– unless they are a rock-like foundation in the life of every staff member.

Lack of integrity in the believing community is nothing new. You can read about it in the story of Gehazi, the personal assistant to the famous prophet Elisha (2 Kings 5:20-27). You will recall that when Naaman, in gratitude for being healed from the scourge of his skin disease, insisted that Elisha took some payment for the ministry he had given, and the prophet refused. Elisha, by refusing the gift, was saying, 'I serve the Lord and I don't need your money.' But Gehazi had other ideas and ran after Naaman and said: 'My boss may have said no but I am happy to take your money.'

All of us can be tempted as Gehazi was – and we need that canopy of God's protection over every part of our 'core values' life together. Never take for granted the values of integrity, truth and freedom. They are values that have to be seen in action. If we are serious about values such as these, we will ask the Lord to open our eyes to see if we are consistent in living by them.

The core value of *integrity* for the Christian organisation will cover the presentation of accounts. It will include a transparency of answers to those who support us. Will it be honest about the authorship of articles and the use of ghost writers in our publicity? Will it avoid the exploitation of people when using photographs in publicity? Will it compensate staff members generously for going the extra mile? Will it regularly review any decisions which involve the use of compromise in difficult circumstances? For example, paying financial backhanders to get medical supplies through customs so that a sick child in a mission hospital lives.

The core value of *truth* for the organisation may require confronting someone senior in the organisation with the news that their ministry effectiveness in an important area has run its course. For the ministry effectiveness of the organisation, a new wineskin structure is needed, and their useful skills need to be used elsewhere.

The core value of *freedom* in the organisation means we ask the questions: we know what the State requests and understand what the law requires. But does there come the moment when what is requested by the State is infringing the freedom of the Lord to lead this organisation? When are there grounds for civil protest and disobedience? Compile your own list of core values – but aim to be distinct. The real distinctive we are aiming for is seeing core values in action.

6. The sixth distinctive is to listen to the voices of the cultures

Set yourself to be a listening-ear organisation before you broadcast your message to the world.

One of the theological tasks of the Church is to penetrate as deeply as possible into the great existential questions that hang over culture. I agree with Wilbert Shenk when he says that to be credible, 'evangelisation must engage a culture intellectually, socially, politically and personally or experientially'. Shenk is right to suggest that: 'The Church is most at risk where it has been present in a culture for a long period of time so that it no longer conceives its relation to culture in terms of a missionary encounter.'[59]

---

59. Wilbert R. Shenk, *Write the Vision: The Church Renewed* (Harrisburg, PA: Trinity Press, 1995), p. 71.

Living in tension with the culture is never an easy task for the Christian organisation, but I like the suggestion of Nigel Wright that we should deal with people on the grounds of a common humanity and the basis of our common questions rather than our differing answers.

This is not to replace the evangelistic challenge by giving priority to the unchanging good news of the gospel. It is a sound missiological principle to prepare the ground. It requires us to be the 'big ears' Christian organisation before we are the broadcasting company. If we listen carefully to our culture, there are common questions for humanity.

There are common questions about eternity. How do we answer a child's question about life after death?

There are common questions for spirituality. Famous people say their lives gave been turned round by reading the book *Cosmic Ordering Service*. The book claims to help you realise all your wishes by placing an order with the universe.[60]

There are common questions for human sexuality. As when the culture assumes you cannot be a whole and healthy person unless you are having sex. There is a great line in the film *Vanilla Sky*[61] when Cameron Diaz says to Tom Cruise: 'Don't you know that when you sleep with someone, your body makes a promise whether you do or not?'

Insights we learn from attentive listening should shape the mission strategy, the programmes and the publicity of the Christian organisation.

---

60. Barbel Mohr, *Cosmic Ordering Service* (London: Hodder & Stoughton, 2006).
61. 2001. Distributed by Paramount Pictures.

7. The seventh and final distinctive is to keep your eye on the big picture.

I remember my late friend Donald English sharing with me that tri-focal vision is exhilarating if you can manage it. Look back, because if we jettison Christian history, the present becomes distorted; look around, because if we neglect what God is doing in the present, life becomes illusory; look ahead, because if we ignore the future God is preparing, hope loses its meaning.

This is the unique distinctive for the Christian organisation. All our planning, dreaming and strategising is within this tri-focal big-picture framework. Someone in your organisation needs to know how to conduct this big-picture symphony. Staff members should be able to hum its melodies.

We do need to *look back* at Christian history and rediscover the ways of God with his people through the centuries.

We need to *look around* at the big picture where God is working through his people. Ask him to open your eyes to see a larger world of fruitful ministries. Most of us work within very narrow parameters and we need the Lord to open our eyes to see where ministry is being done in his name and to his glory (Mark 9:38-41). We cannot side-line completely our preferences and prejudices, but we can ask the Lord to introduce us to new partners in our kingdom work.

And above all, *look forward* to where God is taking us in the future. All our dreaming must be in line with his promises for what is to come. If we want to dissent from the dominant culture of the business world which constructs the world for us, then we need a biblical vision which, in Richard Bauckham's words: 'purges the Christian imagination, refurbishing it with alternative visions of how the world is and will be.'[62] I suggest that regular readings from the book of Revelation provides us with such purging and refurbishment.

John captures his vision in 249 words (Revelation 21:1-8) as he picks up all the colours of God's story and paints a vivid picture of the gospel story in its culmination.

We see how the entire history of the human race has been moving towards this destiny of a perfectly prepared city which is pure and peaceful and filled with the presence of God. And we can experience a foretaste of that perfect city today. We know where our ascended King resides and rules.

We believe with the apostle Paul that Jesus is the glue of the universe – that 'in him all things hold together' (Colossians 1:17). This is where the Lord is leading us ultimately and we should be aiming for nothing less than this excellence.

If you want to be a truly distinctive Christian organisation, then go deeper into the life of the Lord who governs this universe and bring the life of your organisation more fully under his glorious regime.

62. Richard Bauckham, The Theology of the Book of Revelation (Cambridge: Cambridge University Press, 1993), p. 17.

This tribute is to my late friend Jenny Green. I have known her husband, Andrew Green, since he was student at Spurgeon's College in the early 1980s. I was thrilled when he was called to succeed me as senior pastor of Upton Vale, and he was an encouraging and supportive friend during the days when I was engaged in my national ministry with the Baptist Union.

When we retired to Torbay in 2010, it enabled us to renew our fellowship with Jenny and Andrew. His beloved wife, Jenny, endured a five-year battle with cancer and eventually died in October 2018. Andrew and the family invited me to conduct the thanksgiving service for Jenny at Upton Vale Torquay on 19 October 2018.

It was one of the most uplifting thanksgiving services I have ever attended. The family gave the most moving testimonies to the gifted life of Jenny – and the singing of some of her favourite hymns were songs of triumph to her risen and reigning Lord.

I consider Andrew as one of my closest friends, and during the Covid years of 2020-22, we met weekly online to share our mutual love of music, art and poetry.

17

Tribute to a Friend

Jennifer Margaret Wilson was born in Northampton on 18 January 1948. Her father, Jack, was a manager for National Provincial Bank, now known as NatWest. Her mum, Hilda, was very artistic and a stay-at-home mum. Jenny was the middle child with her elder sister, Sue, and her younger brother, Mike. Jack and Hilda had a happy marriage and loved their three children.

In 1958, when Jenny was ten, her father, Jack, moved to Cleveleys in Lancashire as bank manager – and later the family moved to Hambleton, which is on the Fylde coast, about seven miles from Blackpool.

Jenny went to Beech Road Primary School, then Arnold High School for Girls. When she was fifteen, Jenny's RE teacher encouraged a group from the school to attend a Christian conference at Capernwray Hall, Lancashire and it was here that Jenny first committed her life to Jesus Christ, and she remained firm in her Christian faith to the end of her life.

In 1966, she commenced teacher training studies at Elizabeth Gaskell College in Manchester and was part of the Christian Union scene at the University of Manchester.

Once she had qualified, her first teaching posts were in Leicester, where she played hockey for Leicester Ladies and produced all the costumes for the University of Leicester production of *The Duchess of Malfi*.

From 1972-75, Jenny was on the staff of the Inter-Varsity Fellowship (IVF) working in colleges in the north-west of England. At the same time Andrew Green was working for the IVF among the universities of the north-west. Andrew and Jenny first met at a Keswick IVF camp for 250 students – all under canvas! At these IVF camps Jenny was head cook and Andrew was the camp adjutant. An adjutant assists a senior officer which, to my mind, doesn't sound as important a title as head cook!

Andrew and Jenny were both based in Manchester, living just half a mile from each other, so love was destined to blossom, and the happy couple were married on 30 July 1977. They celebrated with great joy their fortieth anniversary in July 2017. It was always a sadness to Jenny that her mum had died in April 1977 and her dad just six weeks later, so neither of her parents saw her married to Andrew.

In time there arrived what Jenny termed her 'three gorgeous children', Anna, Sarah and the self-designated mother's favourite – Simon. In the passage of time love blossomed again and Jonny, Neil and Sarah joined the clan and then came eight adorable grandchildren, Reuben, Theo, Jesse, Jemima, Milly, Annabel, Toby and Eloise. Just three short of a cricket team.

Andrew and Jenny pastored four churches: Poynton Baptist, Cheshire, Cross Street Baptist, Islington while Andrew was a student at Spurgeon's College, Bookham Baptist, Surrey and then Upton Vale Baptist, Torquay where Andrew was senior minister for twenty-five years from

1989-2014. During most of the Torquay years Jenny was teaching, first at South Devon College then fourteen years at Westlands School. And in all these years she served as a wonderful mother to her three children.

I know I can speak on behalf of the Upton Vale family by recording that the twenty-five years here at Upton Vale were amazingly fruitful years of faithful ministry and pastoral care, with scores of friendships fostered by the legendary open-house hospitality practised by the Green family.

Jenny brought a creative commitment to the Upton Vale Cottage Café, where unsuspecting customers became guinea pigs for a Mary Berry recipe from her latest book. Jenny was a keen needlewoman and a gifted designer and not long after arriving in Torquay, she press-ganged a small like-minded group of women to make banners to beautify the church, and you can see some of those banners on display today. Her gifts as a quilter were a blessing to many new mums who would receive a beautiful baby bag or cot quilt made by Jenny.

She joined a local patchwork and quilting group in 1993 and enlivened the group with humour and friendship. Jenny's cakes were an essential part of the class, and those who were conscious of expanding waistlines were unreliably informed by Jenny there were no calories in her cake recipes!

Jenny had high standards for Upton Vale catering teams which she led, whether it was church functions or the Cottage Café – all presentation had to confirm to Mrs Green's exacting standards. I can reveal that today's catering team were most conscious to meet the high standards set by their team captain, Jenny. So when you enter the Lymington Room after the service for refreshments please note:

There is plenty of parsley around the sandwiches.
There will be fresh doilies on the plates.
There are definitely no paper cups on display.
Turquoise blue napkins are available – Jenny's
favourite colour.

Jenny Green played a full part in the ministry of this church, not least by her loving support and encouragement of Andrew. Jenny was God's special gift to Andrew and she knew that Andrew had landed in her life as a gift from the Lord. They were a true love match and complemented and completed each other. Andrew can be cautious – Jenny was always confident. Andrew might ponder anxiously all the possible outcomes for an event, while Jenny boldly stated, 'You'll be fine.'

Jenny had the ability to let things go, which made her a perfect friend to those who worry and are anxious. Jenny would shrug her shoulders at a challenge and just let it go, saying, 'It'll be OK' –and mostly it was! I loved Jenny's forthrightness and plain-speaking and you never had to guess what she was thinking. I can hear her on my shoulder this afternoon pleading: 'Please say something about my weaknesses, David.'

Alright, let's list them.

She refused to make rice pudding for Andrew. He was dependent on handouts from Monday lunches and kind-hearted church members, who took pity on him.

I think we would all agree Jenny was not great on timekeeping. There is an apocryphal tale that Jenny was late for a wedding service, but as the bride was running thirty minutes late it meant Jenny arrived ten minutes early. More accurate is the wedding service where the bride was ten minutes late, and Jenny arrived nine minutes late and threw herself into a vacant seat and in a loud whisper said, 'The wedding can now commence.'

Jenny may have been a great cook but, compared to Andrew, she didn't know how to load the dishwasher. With his love of liturgy, Andrew knew every cup and plate had its proper place!

She was a member of her house group for twenty-one years and I am reliably told by an anonymous source that Jenny was often on the naughty sofa during Bible studies as there was always much chattering taking place wherever she was sitting.

She will be missed at the house group croquet parties where she blatantly cheated, claiming on biblical grounds that she was no longer living under law.

Jenny didn't appreciate culture in the same way as her husband. If there was a programme choice on television between the history of art BBC 4 or another showing of the film *Sleepless in Seattle* on ITV, we all know what Jenny would choose.

Much to Andrew's disappointment, with his vast knowledge of art galleries, Jenny would declare: 'If you have seen one art gallery, you've seen them all.' They were once on holiday in Venice and Jenny was not terribly enthusiastic to visit St Mark's Basilica as, in Jenny's mind, it was just another pile of old stones.

That is, until she got inside St Mark's where she discovered the floor of the church is a marble carpet spread over no less than 2,000m. The different-colour marble creates the most varied geometric shapes and the designer in Jenny was enthralled by the intricate beauty on display. Jenny was a spiritually mature woman who knew this was a moment to praise the Lord of design, colour and beauty. This is why Christians praise God from the glories of his creation to the wonders of his salvation.

This may be the appropriate moment to express our thanks to Andrew for his numerous postings on Caring Bridge. His regular diary brought a host of friends up-to-date with news of Jenny's progress in health and enabled us to be informed as prayer supporters. Jenny began her long battle with cancer five and half years ago when the family began to use Caring Bridge.[63]

The postings were often inspiring and spiritually uplifting and provided us with a glimpse of your faith and trust in the Lord. In the last days of Jenny's earthly life, there was a wonderful posting from a friend of the family where she spoke of heaven, borrowing words from *The Valley of Vision*:

I live here as a fish in a vessel of water,
Only enough to keep me alive.
But in heaven, I shall swim in the ocean.
Here I have a little air to keep me breathing,
But there I shall have sweet and fresh gales.[64]

Jenny is now safe, home in heaven. We read earlier from the book of Revelation which terms heaven as the land of no more. There is no more suffering, pain or tears. But alongside the no more, we need to put the much more. Jenny hasn't lost – she has gained, because as the Word says: 'To live is Christ and to die is gain' (Philippians 1:21).

Jenny is now with Christ. She is with the Lord she followed faithfully for fifty-five years and is now experiencing the ministry of the Good Shepherd who promised rest and

63. www.caringbridge.org (accessed 10.5.23) is an online charitable organisation that enables family and friends to post messages of encouragement when a loved one is undergoing medical treatment.
64. Arthur Bennett, ed, *The Valley of Vision: A Collection of Puritan Prayer and Devotions* (Edinburgh: Banner of Truth, 2012).

refreshment by 'still waters' (Psalm 23:3, ESV). When you ponder the 'much more' of heaven as Jenny did in her final days of pain and suffering, who wouldn't want to be there?

I can hear Jenny saying to us this afternoon: 'Follow me to the place where I have gone and trust my Saviour Jesus for all you are worth.'

Prayer of thanksgiving for the life of Jenny

Heavenly Father, we thank you for your steadfast love that never ceases
And your compassion that never fails.
We celebrate your goodness in the life of Jenny.
We thank you for her parents, Jack and Hilda
Who cared for Jenny in her growing years.
For family life together with Sue and Mike.
We thank you for bringing Jenny to faith in the Lord Jesus Christ.
For the many gifts and abilities in her life
That were freely used in your service.
Thank you for her down-to-earth practical faith without frills.
For her solid persevering in Christian discipleship.
For everything in her life that reflected the image of Christ.
For her courage in the face of suffering.
For giving Jenny a peaceful heart in her final days.
For granting her faith to stand on the promises of God, trusting you to guide her safely home to heaven.
We pray for Jenny's family today.
Continue your comfort and support to them.
Thank you for Andrew's loving devotion and care for Jenny,

for raising up this family as an example of faith under trial
that, in spite of their pain and grief,
they bear a bold witness to Jesus as the resurrection
and the life.
We commend to your loving care Andrew,
Anna and Jonny – Reuben, Theo and Jesse,
Sarah and Neil – Jemima, Milly and Annabel,
Simon and Sarah – Toby and Eloise.
Strengthen the hearts of the older ones.
Inspire the younger ones with the example
of their grandmother's faith and love for you.
Finally, we pray for ourselves.
May all of us make a fresh commitment to your service.
May our thanksgiving for the life of Jenny
show itself in a readiness to be faithful to your will.
Deal gently with those of us who find faith a mystery.
Help us to read more clearly than ever
the good news of Jesus in the life of Jenny.
So may the love of Jesus draw us to himself,
the power of Jesus strengthen us in his service,
the joy of the Lord Jesus fill our lives,
to the glory of his name.
Amen.

My brother, Ian, and his wife, Ruth, celebrated their twenty-fifth wedding anniversary on 3 August 1999. It was held in the beautiful grounds of Ashby Folville Manor, Leicestershire, the home of their close friends, Mike and Rosemary. Janet and I cherish our friendship with Ian and Ruth and their four sons and their families.

As the basis for my talk, I chose to use the story of Jesus, who was a guest at the wedding in Cana, as told in the Gospel of John, chapter 2.

The wedding at Cana is one of the most famous in history, yet we don't even know the name of the bride or the groom. But I imagined the couple in John 2 sending a greeting to Ian and Ruth as they celebrated their twenty-fifth anniversary.

The anniversary celebration would prove a historic event for two children. In 2022 our daughter, Niki, was looking through photo albums and came across a group photo of Ian and Ruth's twenty-fifth anniversary. She saw our grandson Sam, aged three, perched on his dad's shoulders. Later she realised in the front row was a young Katie Brown, aged six, standing near to her mother, Debbie, my brother, Ian's, personal assistant.

That day in 1999, Sam and Katie didn't meet each other. But twenty-three years later, Sam and Katie were married in St Aldate's, Oxford. They used the 1999 photo as a feature in their wedding invitation.

The sermon I gave at their wedding is in Chapter 13.

18

Marriage Wisdom

The most important thing we remember about our special day is that Jesus came as a guest to our wedding. Most of the religious leaders we knew when we got married appeared more concerned about making sure the rituals were observed, and were adept at spotting rain clouds rather than sunrises. Wedding receptions filled with joy and laughter, where the wine flowed freely, were not their scene. We wrongly thought that if God's representatives were not too happy about marriage, then God was probably feeling the same way. When our eyes were opened to discover the identity of Jesus and we realised that God's Son was one of our wedding guests, this affirmed God's grace-filled blessing on our marriage.

Through the years we've discovered the rich blessings God intends for married couples and how much practical wisdom he shares in his book. You may smile when you read in Proverbs: 'Grey hair is a crown of splendour; it is attained by a righteous life.'[65] But all married couples need wise words to strengthen their relationship. You will

---

65. See Proverbs 16:31, NIV 1984.

discover the advice to be 'quick to listen, slow to speak'[66] is proven wisdom for marriage, and the ear is often a better gift than the mouth.

Jesus certainly changed our view of religion. We had both been brought up to believe in God and knew the history of our faith tradition. We loved the joy and celebration of the occasional festivals of faith, which were wonderful times for a gathering of family and friends. But for everyday living, we found it wearisome having to observe numerous rules and requirements.

We confess the last thing a bride and groom needed at their reception is six huge stone water jars as a centrepiece. Try blending them into the floral display! But our parents insisted the water pots were part of the ritualistic way of religious life that we had to observe. What a good job we had followed the religious tradition, as it was a most dramatic moment when the 500 litres of water in the jars was suddenly transformed into quality vintage wine. We were grateful that the wine supply had been restored and an embarrassing situation avoided, especially for the groom.

The deeper meaning of Jesus changing the water into wine became clearer when sometime after our wedding we became his followers. It was then we realised the watery basis of our religious faith had been keeping all those religious rites and following all those regulations – whereas the new wine of the kingdom, which Jesus had inaugurated, was enjoying a close personal relationship with God. The change in our lives was immediately apparent. A worship service became a meeting with God; prayer was a personal conversation with God; reading the ancient Scriptures was not a burdensome duty, but an opportunity to hear God

---

66. See James 1:19.

speaking to us. We were aware of God's presence in our home and could sense him whispering in our ears, 'This is the right way to go.'

Some of our guests were offended by an exchange of words between Jesus and his mother. Mary was a member of the catering team organising the reception and she realised the seriousness of the situation when it became obvious we were running out of wine.

His mother knew the divine capabilities of Jesus and she thought he should be aware of the developing panic behind the scenes. When she told Jesus that there was no more wine for the guests, implying he needed to do something, Jesus responded by saying: 'Dear woman, let me handle this my way.'[67]

The more we reflected on the exchange between Mary and Jesus, we discovered another teaching moment for our marriage. There have been many occasions when we've been caught in the tension between duty to each other and our responsibilities to God. We soon discovered the Lord was the third person in our relationship. When conflicts arose, there could be no forgiveness and reconciliation without God's help. We needed *his* wisdom to distinguish between authentic dependence on one another, and the freedom to develop a life with Jesus as individuals.

What Jesus did at our wedding reception was to transform our view of the ordinary and mundane. We can still recall snippets of conversations we had with our guests. One couple who saw the water turned into wine were inspired to comment, 'You two did the ordinary, and you left Jesus to do the miracle.'

The 'ordinary' referred to the back-breaking task of transporting litres of water to fill the stone water jars. We've

---

67. See John 2:4.

repeatedly seen this principle at work in our marriage. Just doing the ordinary things well. We love offering hospitality, and when we do the laborious task of preparing food and inviting the guests, we discover the unseen presence of Jesus in our home does the rest.

In every area of our working lives, we tried to follow the principle of doing the ordinary things and leaving the miracles to Jesus.

Our faith was certainly deepened as a result of the miracle Jesus performed at our wedding reception. We understand your receptions only last a few hours, whereas in our culture they go on for days, and often food, drink and accommodation have to be provided for up to a week!

A bridegroom's reputation is at stake if the supply of food and wine runs out. He cannot be considered a wealthy man able to support his wife if this occurs. Within our friendship circle, one bridegroom was sued by the bride's relatives because of a poor wedding reception. You can appreciate our sense of helplessness when the news came through about the wine supply. We anticipated some 'bad hair days' in our marriage, but not on day one! However, the experience has left a positive mark on our marriage. Every time we feel helpless and anxious, we just remember the advice Mary gave to the best man and his helpers: 'Do whatever Jesus tells you.'[68]

This has been a watchword for our life together and it has not let us down so far.

You would expect us to say something about 'the best wine being saved to the end'. We had followed the custom of every bride and groom and served the choicest vintage wine first. You do this because first impressions count, and

68. See John 2:5.

you want to impress your guests. Besides, as the week of celebrations unfolds, the guests become jaded with so much food and drink and their tastebuds are not so sensitive.

This is why the miracle left such a deep impression, and the best man made his famous comment about 'keeping the best quality wine until the end'.[69] Regularly we have noticed that just when we had enjoyed God's best for our lives, there was so much more he had to give us. As you grow old together, you will be asking the question, 'Does the best wine come at the end?' We can assure you there is an ample supply of vintage wine as you grow older!

There is an ancient tradition in some cultures where a bride and groom wear crowns on their wedding day. The spiritual meaning is the crowns symbolise the couple are a king and queen in a little outpost of God's kingdom.

The day Jesus was a guest at our wedding, we felt we were honourable members of God's royal family, and through all the years of our marriage his goodness has never left us, and we constantly feel the rich favour of God on our lives.

We leave you with the words of an ancient prayer that was said at our wedding.

Ian and Ruth,
The LORD bless you and keep you:
The LORD make his face shine upon you,
and be gracious to you:
The LORD lift his countenance upon you,
and give you peace.[70]
Amen

---

69. See John 2:10.
70. Numbers 6:24-26, RSV.

Articles

I was invited by the editor of the Baptist Ministers' Journal (BMJ) to name the three books I would choose to take to a desert island. The journal was running a series on this theme and my article was published in July 2012. Eleven years on, I would compile a different list of books.

The final book on music has been displaced by Gramophone magazine online editions, but assuming I have no internet access on the island, my old volume of The Gramophone Classical Music Guide will be a trusty companion. The article is reprinted by permission of the editor of BMJ.[71]

---

71. Edited for the purposes of the book.

19

Desert Island Books

When I shared with my family that I had been invited to select three volumes as my desert island books, the big question was whether my absence from home would be during the football or the cricket season? Despite an abiding passion for both sports, neither pastime features in my final choice of books. After some delightful meandering through dozens of possible choices, I have chosen three juggernauts whose combined weight amounts to nearly 10kg with a total number of 3,254 pages. With all this excess baggage, I must have an agreement with the *BMJ* editor that my chosen reading is waiting for me on the desert island!

My first choice is *The Times Comprehensive Atlas of the World*,[72] the world's most prestigious and authoritative atlas. It is acclaimed as the greatest atlas on earth and the ultimate starting point for planning any adventure. Maps fascinate me as I have visited dozens of countries on six of the seven continents, and I am open to suggestions on how

---

72. *The Times Comprehensive Atlas of the World* (NY: Times Books, 2021) The sixteenth edition is published in September 2023.

I can obtain a preaching invitation from the frozen acres of Antarctica! What a beautiful experience it is to turn the pages of this Lamborghini of an atlas, and the naming of every country with its national flag, capital city and date of independence is a cruciverbalist's delight.

My leisure time on the island will be to trace the hundreds of places I have visited – and recall the people I have met during my global travels.

I will retrace the road from Dimapur to Kohima in Nagaland and recall a scary drive on a winding dirt track early on a Sunday morning as we drove to church.

Locating Kinshasa, Lisala and Pimu will bring back memories of a visit to the Democratic Republic of Congo and a boat ride on the river Congo when the temperature was 43C.

Finding the route the bullet train takes from Shanghai to Hangzhou will refresh the inspiration of visiting the 5,000-seater Chongyi Church.

Tracking the Chilean coast road from Santiago to Valparaiso, I will visualise the vineyards and coastal fish restaurants of this port city, termed the 'jewel of the Pacific'.

I will relive the scenic drive down the Great Ocean Road south of Melbourne.

I will trace the sprawling miles of Kazakhstan and recall a December journey through the ice-packed roads of Almaty.

Locating the Bay of Fundy in Nova Scotia, I can still visualise huge flocks of migrating sandpipers using the mudflats as feeding grounds en route to South America.

The map of Armenia will revive nightmares of a hair-raising night-time journey with a 'mad' pastor driving from Tbilisi to Yerevan.

Locating the border crossing between Hungary and Serbia will bring back memories of visiting families in war-torn Novi Sad a few weeks after NATO bombs had destroyed the roads and bridges of the city.

During my daily devotions, I plan to use the atlas as a prayer diary choosing a country per day when I can recall churches I have visited and pastors I count as personal friends. The CPC countries (countries of particular concern) listed by Human Rights Watch will have a particular prayer focus as I remember the 250 million believers in sixty countries denied their basic human right of religious liberty.

My second book is *A History of Christianity: The First Three Thousand Years* by Diarmaid MacCulloch.[73] I have chosen this volume for the expertise of the author who is an extremely impressive polymath with an extraordinary range of knowledge in numerous subject areas.

I am in awe of this mammoth work, and it intrigues me that the author describes himself as a candid friend of Christianity and in the preface dedicates the book to Philip Kennedy: 'Faithful friend, who has managed to persist in affirming a Christian story.' MacCulloch was brought up in a Suffolk parsonage and depicts his father as a man with a high view of episcopacy but a low view of bishops. He says his book is church history from the rectory window.

He questions Christian faith: 'I live with the puzzle of wondering how something so apparently crazy can be so captivating to millions of other members of my species.'[74] I love his description of the Gospels: 'These Christian books are an unusually "downmarket" variety of biography, in which ordinary people reflect on their experience of Jesus, where the powerful and beautiful stand on the side-lines of the story and where it is often the poor, the ill-educated

73. Diarmaid MacCulloch, *A History of Christianity: The First Three Thousand Years* (London: Allen Lane, 2009).
74. Ibid., p.11.

and the disreputable whose encounters with God are most vividly described.'[75]

The ninety-two pages of footnotes and suggestions for further reading is a continual feast, although reading these pages on a desert island will be frustrating with no online access to library facilities. The book is rich in theological debates, prayers, hymn lines and pithy quotes that will keep me stimulated between collecting water and stockpiling wood for the fire.

I have lived with this book since it was published, and tucked inside my copy is a review by Rowan Williams. It's an appreciative critique that you can find on *The Guardian* website[76] and provides an insight into what an Oxford tutorial must have been like with Archbishop Rowan. When I am rescued from my desert island, I will request an afternoon with Professor MacCulloch. I will first thank him for his spirit of generosity to all traditions in this magnum opus, and then humbly provide him with evidence for including an even stronger English Free-Church perspective to his revised edition of the book.

My third book is *The Gramophone Classical Music Guide (GCMG)*. I have subscribed to the *Gramophone* magazine for more than forty years and this annual is considered the most authoritative guide to the best classical recordings by the world's leading music critics. It has brief biographies of major composers from Adams to Zemlinsky and compares the best recordings with star ratings.

From my childhood, music has been my constant love and inspiration – and most days I am listening to music streamed from the digital music service Spotify. My earliest

---

75. Ibid., p.77.
76. www.theguardian.com/books/2009/sep/19/history-christianity-diarmaid-mccullouch (accessed 24.4.23).

memories of musical influence include piano lessons with Marjorie Hellyer who accurately prophesied that my ability to play anything by ear would hamper my discipline of sight-reading.

I enjoyed membership in the junior school choir that was led enthusiastically by my music master, Geoffrey Tristram, the organist at Christchurch Priory, Dorset. I recall memorable visits in the late 1940s to the Bournemouth Winter Gardens for concerts by the Bournemouth Municipal Orchestra (later the BSO), which was building a national reputation under its Austrian conductor Rudolf Schwarz, who had been a prisoner in the Nazi concentration camp of Belsen. But my burgeoning musical career came off the rails in St Andrew's Presbyterian Church, Bournemouth when I fell off the piano stool during an exam and the examiner kindly recorded: 'This piece had vitality in spite of one slight stumble!'

I have selected for my luxury item on the desert island a 64GB iPad where I hope to have stored some of my favourite music albums (more eclectic than the classical résumé which follows).

I will relish reading the critics notes in the *GCMG* as I listen to the spiritually intense 'A German Requiem' by Brahms (Otto Klemperer version) and recall the personal spiritual roots to Eric Whitacre's 'Water Night' that enhances the listening experience of his music. His adaptation of e.e. Cummings poem: 'I Thank You God for Most This Amazing Day', would be a perfect way to start an early morning biblical reflection on the island.[77]

For the end of the day, I might select Tchaikovsky's invitation to worship with his heart-stopping 'Liturgy of

---

77. Eric Whitacre, www.ericwhitacre.com (accessed 10.5.23); and a link to e.e. cummings reading his poem.

St John Chrysostom', and if I need an adrenaline rush, I will choose the mercurial performance of Rachmaninov's 'Piano Concerto No. 3' with Martha Argerich's seismic final movement.

If I am feeling morose then the 'Adagio' from the Schubert *String Quintet in C Major*, Elgar's 'Elegy for Strings' or his 'Cello Concerto in E Minor' (du Pré's EMI 1965 recording) will be a soothing consolation and remind me of friends who suffer from long-term depression who testify that when words fail to get through, then music speaks to the soul in the valley of despair.

For the Christian festivals, I would select one of the Bach cantatas from the outstanding Bach Cantata Pilgrimage arranged by John Eliot Gardiner.[78] This ambitious project recorded all 198 surviving cantatas by J.S. Bach and was accomplished in one year with fifty-nine concerts performed in fifty cities in thirteen countries. I often play these discs for spiritual inspiration when I have a writing project.

Having devoured this compendious music guide, I hope I would emerge from the island with the capacity to share my new-found knowledge on lesser-known Polish composers like Henryk Wieniawski and Tadeusz Szeligowski!

As I prepare to head to my desert island, I am collecting ideas and stories that will bring inspiration and encouragement, and I share one from the collection. A traveller is stranded for several months on a small desert island in the middle of the Pacific Ocean – and one day notices a bottle in the sand with a piece of paper in it: 'Due to lack of maintenance', he reads, 'we regretfully have had to cancel your email account.'

---

78. www.montiverdi.co.uk (accessed 10.5.23).

Visiting Billy Graham at his Montreat mountainside home

This was a Baptist World article in January 2008 and is reprinted by permission.[79]

I was privileged to attend Billy's funeral on Friday, 2 March 2018. He died aged ninety-nine on 21 February. Two thousand people gathered in a tent outside the Billy Graham Library in Charlotte, North Carolina to pay their final respects to the man known as 'America's Pastor'.

He had enjoyed personal audiences with twelve consecutive presidents from Harry Truman to Barack Obama and was particularly close to Lyndon B. Johnson and Richard Nixon.

Billy once said, 'I am not going to Heaven because I have preached to great crowds or read the Bible many times. I'm going to Heaven just like the thief on the cross who said in that last moment: "Lord, remember me."'[80]

79. Edited for the purposes of this book.
80. www.brainyquote.com/quotes/billy_graham_626328 (accessed 23.5.23).

20

A Tribute to Dr Billy Graham on His Ninetieth Birthday

I was just one among the 120,000 well-wishers who sent Dr Billy Graham a personal greeting on his ninetieth birthday on 7 November 2008. He celebrated this milestone birthday at a private barbecue near his mountain home in North Carolina.

He recorded a message to his many friends and said: 'I've learned that these latter years can be some of the most fulfilling of our lives. I am grateful for each day; thankful for the measure of health I have and am overwhelmed by this celebration.'

In my personal greeting I thanked Billy Graham for being a shaping influence in each decade of my life.

In the 1940s, when I was eight years old, he visited my home church in Winton, Bournemouth. My late father, Arthur Coffey, was one of the British pastors who invited him to visit England when Billy was a young evangelist with the organisation, Youth for Christ. I can't recall the message he preached at my local church, but I have a distinct memory of the excitement his preaching generated in the congregation.

In 1954, London was the venue of his first international crusade. Billy preached in the Harringay Arena seventy-two times over twelve weeks, sharing the gospel with crowds totalling more than 2 million, of whom 38,000 came forward to make decisions for Jesus Christ. I was thirteen when I made my first public commitment to Jesus Christ at this London Crusade. I had never doubted the truth of the good news of the gospel, but it was Billy's preaching that brought me to a distinct moment of commitment to Jesus Christ, fifty-four years ago.

During the 1960s, I was a student at Spurgeon's College – and recall my college principal, Dr George Beasley Murray, returning a changed man from the Berlin Congress on Evangelism. He shared with the students that he had been challenged by Billy Graham to be more intentionally evangelistic in his preaching ministry. It was deeply impressive to hear a world-famous New Testament scholar give his testimony as to how God had challenged him through an evangelism conference.

It was in Stockholm, Sweden, at the Baptist World Congress in 1975 that I heard Billy preach to thousands at the final open-air service of the congress. His preaching that day was a reminder that we don't need to make the gospel relevant – we simply demonstrate its relevance by preaching the message of the Bible with spiritual power and authority.

Attending Mission England in May 1984, God revitalised my ministry as a pastor and enabled me to enter a new era of doing 'the work of an evangelist' (2 Timothy 4:5). On a Saturday afternoon at Bristol City stadium [Ashton Gate], I was overwhelmed with emotion as I witnessed hundreds of people streaming forward in response to Billy's invitation to follow Christ. This experience challenged me as a local church pastor to be more persuasive in my preaching, and during the succeeding years, I have seen a greater harvest of people coming to Christ through my preaching ministry.

In the mid-1990s, I had the immense privilege of accompanying Dr Denton Lotz and Dr Nilson Fanini on a private visit to Dr and Mrs Graham in their mountain home in Montreat, North Carolina, and the memory of their gracious hospitality and fellowship lives with me to this day. The recently published autobiography of David Frost was on their coffee table and Billy opened the book to reveal it was a signed copy by the author. The inscription read: 'To my friend Billy who is a recurring theme in this book and in my life'. Billy then shared a number of examples of how David Frost had given him opportunities to share the gospel on television programmes he was hosting.

In the first year of the new millennium, I was one of the 10,000 delegates to the Amsterdam 2000 conference organised by the Billy Graham Evangelistic Association organisation. Once again, I was inspired and challenged from the feast of teaching and fellowship. The conference was planned to be an event when Billy's peer group passed on the responsibility of international Christian leadership to a new generation of younger global leaders. The only shadow over the gathering was the absence of Billy and Ruth Graham owing to their frail health.

Although Billy Graham's public ministry has ceased, his wisdom is still available. Billy reportedly told his friends on his ninetieth birthday: 'I know how to die but nobody ever taught me how to grow old.' I am reminded of the words of John Bunyan:

Thou must run a long and tedious journey before you come to the land of promise . . . perseverance is a greater part of the cross.[81]

Billy Graham is God's long-distance journeyman who knows that grace is gradually leading him home. He has been a mentor to all of us in the spirit of Hebrews 13:8 and I record my deep and lasting appreciation to God for his life and ministry.

---

81. John Bunyan, *The Heavenly Footman* (Scotts Valley, CA: CreateSpace Independent Publishing Platform, 2015). Originally published 1698.

Meeting with King Abdullah II of Jordan

This article for Baptist World was published November 2007 and is reprinted by permission.[82]

My journey to Jordan was the most significant encounter I had with Muslims during my time as president.

During this visit to King Abdullah II, I met his cousin, Prince Ghazi, who had authored in October 2007 an open letter signed by 138 Muslim scholars entitled: 'A Common Word Between Us and You' (ACW[83]).

The letter was a call for peace from Muslim leaders to Christians leaders and tried to find common ground for understanding between both world religions.

On behalf of the BWA, I responded in October 2007 with an initial welcome to ACW. This was followed by an extensive theological response in December 2008, much of the scholarly work was contributed by Dr Paul Fiddes.

82. Edited for the purposes of this book.
83. www.acommonword.com/(accessed 26.4.23).

21

Talking With Muslims

Let me share a story of two men called Abdullah. One man is His Royal Highness, King Abdullah II of Jordan. The other Abdullah hires horses out to tourists in the ancient city of Petra.

King Abdullah II of Jordan granted me an audience during a recent visit to the Middle East when our delegation shared with him the concerns of Jordanian Baptists for full religious liberty and recognition by the State. We congratulated the king on his eloquent address to the US Congress and shared our mutual concerns for peace in the Middle East. The king gave advance notice that thirty-eight moderate Muslim scholars were writing an open letter to the Pope, and the leadership of the Baptist World Alliance would be included as named recipients of this significant letter. The king shared that without peace and justice between Christians and Muslims there can be no meaningful peace in the world. We are now in receipt of the open letter from the Muslim scholars – and the Baptist World Alliance is consulting on a considered response to the important issues raised in the letter.

I met the other Abdullah during a visit to the ancient city of Petra. I had walked the hot and dusty trail into the heart of this amazing rose-red city half as old as time – and felt I had stumbled on to the film set of *Indiana Jones and the Last Crusade*. I opted to hire a horse for the return journey, which was how I met Abdullah. His first question to me was: 'Are you a Christian?' which was swiftly followed by the enquiry: 'Why aren't you a Muslim?'

My answer to his friendly questions were returned while balancing on the back of a horse – my first time in the saddle for more than thirty years! Abdullah was passionate about sharing his Islamic faith and I was sending up arrow prayers as I shared with him the reason for the hope I have in Jesus Christ (1 Peter 3:15).

My encounter with two men called Abdullah was a reminder that talking with Muslims presents us with an opportunity to hear their concerns as well as express freely our own faith in Jesus Christ. I suggest that the following should shape our conversations:

1) We need a bold humility in sharing what our Christian faith means to us. When there is a meeting of different faiths, it requires every party to be faithful to their own convictions and respectful of others.

2) We need to give greater attention to mentioning the Bible in our conversations. Other faith traditions have a place of honour for their sacred Scriptures and frequently quote from a relevant passage. When Christians fail to do this, it appears we do not honour our own holy Scriptures.

3) We need to be unafraid to confess our sins. Christian history includes bloody crusades and inquisitions,

social intolerance and intellectual bigotry. Vinoth Ramachandra suggests that any sharing of the gospel has to begin with the humble acknowledgement of betrayals of the gospel by the Church itself.

4) We need to be truthful about the woeful lack of religious liberty in Muslim states. It is morally wrong for Islamic regimes to subscribe to the UN Declaration of Human Rights and prohibit freedom of religious worship and conversion among their citizens. And it is doubly hypocritical for their citizens to enjoy those rights when living in a foreign country while denying the same liberty to foreigners living in their home country.

5) We need to demonstrate the virtues and graces of Christian discipleship in the power of the Holy Spirit. In the history of the Church, the most fruitful witness is always the demonstration of humbly following Jesus with a spirit of joyful and loving service.

In a recent survey conducted at Fuller Seminary California, 750 Muslims who have decided to follow Christ were invited to answer an extensive questionnaire based on the single question: 'What attracts Muslims to follow Jesus?' The majority of those Muslims responding ranked the lifestyle of Christians as the most important influence in their decision to follow Christ.[84]

In the words of St Francis of Assisi: 'It is no use walking anywhere to preach unless our walking is our preaching.'[85]

84. Jennifer Riley, 'Why Muslims Follow Jesus', *Christianity Today*, 24 October 2007, www.christianitytoday.com (accessed 10.5.23).
85. Francis of Assisi (1181-1226), www.brainyquote.com/quotes/francis_of_assisi_153347 (accessed 26.4.23).

Planning meeting Lambeth Palace

I served as the Free Churches' moderator and a co-president of Churches Together in England (2003-07). The four presidents met regularly at Lambeth Palace for prayer, fellowship and discussion on major national issues.

At one of our meetings, we had been invited to sign a letter to the Israeli ambassador to the UK expressing our deep concern for the plight of Christians living in the Holy Land.

We agreed that, rather than send yet another letter, we would travel together to Israel and Palestine and show solidarity with our brothers and sisters. I count this visit as one of the most memorable of my journeys to the Middle East. The article appeared in the Baptist Times early in 2007 and is reproduced by permission.[86]

It is important to check the current statistics for Bethlehem. At the beginning of 2023, there was an intensification of violence between Israel and the Palestinians, with deaths mounting on both sides. For a current insight into the situation see the article by Tim Livesey, CEO of Embrace the Middle East. I am one of the patrons of this charity.[87]

86. Edited for the purposes of this book.
87. Tim Livesey, 'What is Going on in Israel and Palestine', *The Church of England Newspaper*, 23 April 2023.

22

Six Days in the Holy Land at Christmas

Tuesday, 19 December 2006

It is said that Pope John Paul II once declared that two solutions were possible to the Palestinian-Israeli conflict – the realistic and the miraculous. The realistic would involve a divine intervention, the miraculous, a voluntary agreement between the two parties.

Doubtless an apocryphal story, but it captures the political impasse of one of the longest-running conflicts in the world. Caught up in this conflict are Israeli and Arab Christian communities who feel isolated and forgotten and the purpose of the Churches Together in England (CTE) pilgrimage is to show solidarity with the Christians of the Holy Land who live at the heart of this unending warfare, especially those who live in the beleaguered town of Bethlehem.

The four presidents of CTE took the preliminary decision in June 2006 that, diaries permitting, they would visit 'the living stones'[88] of Jerusalem and Bethlehem prior to Christmas. It is a minor miracle that busy diaries were

---

88. See 1 Peter 2:5.

273

eventually coordinated and we were able to make an act of solidarity with the suffering Church.

The final day of preparation included deciding which music I would store on my iPod, and I chose John Taverner's *Lament for Jerusalem*. Taverner's lament is rooted in the grim tradition of a broken-hearted people longing for the day when peace shall come to a bloodstained land. The lament draws together appropriately texts from the three great religious traditions associated with the Holy Land, but the recurring motif is the haunting refrain based in Luke 19:41; Jesus wept and still weeps for Jerusalem.

Wednesday, 20 December 2006

We gathered for prayer in St George's Chapel at London Heathrow Airport at 6 a.m. The Heathrow chaplaincy team prepared a brief service of readings and prayers for our journey. We sang the Advent hymn 'O Come, O Come, Emmanuel'[89] – and lit four candles in front of the Nativity scene.

Considering the passenger chaos that was about to descend on a fog-bound Heathrow, we were grateful that our flight was only two hours delayed. Our late arrival in Israel meant we had kept the Jerusalem heads of churches waiting for two hours at the Greek Orthodox Patriarchate, but as one of the church leaders commented, 'We have spent longer in each other's company than some would have expected – but your late arrival has proved providential for unexpected fellowship!'

---

89. Translated into English by John Mason Neale (1818-66).

Although Baptists and evangelicals are not normally included in the heads of churches meetings, my Baptist Union colleague Graham Sparkes and I had requested that two of our Baptist leaders received invitations to the opening reception and dinner, and I was delighted to greet personally Fuad Haddad who chairs the Association of Baptist churches in Israel, and Bryson Arthur who is heading up the emerging Baptist college in Nazareth.

Thursday, 21 December 2006

This was a day of stark contrasts. The early part of the day was most bleak. First, there was the observation of the biblical scholar who told us: 'I have lived in Jerusalem for forty-five years and these are the worst of times.' Then there was the dearth of visitors to the sacred sites. When we arrived at the Church of the Holy Sepulchre, it was almost deserted. The last time I was in the Holy Land, these sacred sites were packed with visitors. This underlined what was becoming a mantra of despairing voices: 'Where are the pilgrims? Why have they forsaken us? Look what is happening to the Christian community. If we go on declining at the current rate, we will have virtually disappeared by 2015!'

In early afternoon, the panoramic view from the rooftop of the Tantur Ecumenical centre was a shocking introduction to the little town of Bethlehem. This view from the rooftop is a different world to the one described by Phillips Brooks (1835-93) in his nineteenth-century carol, 'O Little Town of Bethlehem'. This little town is not lying still in a 'deep and dreamless sleep' while the 'silent stars' drift by.[90] The 24ft-high security wall overshadowed all my senses as we walked towards the military checkpoint. I felt an overwhelming sense of sadness for the people on both sides of this wall. I felt a welling up of tears and a deep sense of grief for the bloodshed and violence; for the worsening humanitarian crisis in Bethlehem; for the absence of any visible political solution; for the unholy political mess in this sacred space we call the Holy Land.

I know the situation is complex and the high wall reflects the legitimate Israeli security concerns. Half the suicide bombers are said to have come from Bethlehem. But inside this walled community, we came face-to-face with the injustice of the combined effect of the wall, land confiscations and the expanding twenty-seven Israelis settlements in the Bethlehem district. We were told:

- 30 per cent of the population of Bethlehem now lives below the poverty line.
- Unemployment is higher than 25 per cent.
- Pilgrim tourists have traditionally contributed to 65 per cent of Bethlehem's economy.
- In 2000 there were 800,000 visitors.
- In 2005 this had dropped to 274,000 visitors and only a small percentage of these decide to stay overnight in Bethlehem.

As in Jerusalem, the plea from the Christian community is: 'Come and visit us but don't just pass through, please come and stay.'

Our evening dinner was at the Lutheran International Center where Mitri Raheb is the director. Here is a place

---

90. https://hymnary.org/text/o_little_town_of_bethlehem (accessed 26.4.23).

bursting with vision, and it provided the spiritual antidote to the waves of despair I had physically felt throughout the day. We were told by our hosts, don't only look for the pain and suffering in Bethlehem; observe the places where God is bringing life from death – and planting hope where despair has reigned.

In his book *Bethlehem Besieged*,[91] Mitri mentions the glass angels made from the broken bottles and glass found on the streets of Bethlehem. This is the true work of God in Bethlehem. He takes the broken lives of people and makes something beautiful from them.

Friday, 22 December 2006

The day began with communion at 7 a.m. in a tiny cave-like chapel. The rhythmic patterns of prayer and Advent Scripture permeated the whole of the pilgrimage. Our first visit was to Bethlehem University where the bright optimism of the students we met resonated with the mood of last night's dinner.

We joined in a discussion with four students, Aya, Mohammed, Amir and Shatha. They were a very impressive group of Christian and Muslim young people with a shared goal, a vision for a just and peaceful life in Palestine.

Our whirlwind tour of schools and hospitals enabled us to observe the impressive work of the Mar Ephraim primary school and the Bethlehem Arab Society for Rehabilitation. At the St Vincent crèche and the Holy Family maternity hospital I was able to deliver the Christmas cards signed by the children of the school attended by my grandchildren. In

---

91. Mitri Raheb, *Bethlehem Besieged* (Minneapolis, MN: Fortress Press, 2004).

return I received a signed Christmas card for Dr Radcliffe's Church of England School in Oxfordshire. Seventy per cent of Bethlehem babies are born in this remarkable hospital and they also have mobile clinics to reach the poor who live in the remote hillside communities around Bethlehem.

At the end of the day, we gathered in the YMCA Shepherd's Field and under the night sky of Bethlehem we stood around a blazing fire as the Bethlehem Bible College Choir sang carols – and we listened to the feisty words of welcome from their president, Bishara Awad.

It was a joy to meet some of the pastors of local Baptist and Free Evangelical churches. Graham Sparkes had worked hard prior to the visit obtaining email addresses and this paid dividends. It is obvious that in both Jerusalem and Bethlehem these pastors are normally excluded from church leader gatherings, and I sensed they were deeply grateful to have been included in our itinerary.

Bishara Awad presented each of the four pilgrims with a copy of Brother Andrew's book *Light Force*. The book concludes with the words Bishara used in his welcome to the presidents: 'Palestinian believers aren't asking for much – just a little room in your hearts. Don't stop loving Israel but love us as well. Isn't there room in our hearts for both?' [92]

Saturday, 23 December 2006

Following breakfast, we greeted a delegation from Open Bethlehem, the organisation that campaigns to focus world attention on Bethlehem's plight. Their CEO, Leila

---

92. Brother Andrew, *Light Force: A Stirring Account of the Church Caught in the Middle East Crossfire* (Ada, MI: Revell, 2004), p. 318.

Sansour, presented each of the four pilgrims with a Bethlehem passport. Until now, only Pope Benedict had been a recipient of this passport. In receiving the passport, we pledged to be a voice for the voiceless and promised to speak about Bethlehem on our travels and remember the people of this city who long to travel in dignity and freedom.

Returning to Jerusalem, we visited St George's Anglican Cathedral for a short service and a welcome from the retiring Bishop Riah. I had met him on two previous occasions, including the visit of Church leaders to 10 Downing Street prior to the Iraq War. The message to Tony Blair on that occasion was: 'Prime Minister, please remember the road to Baghdad leads through Jerusalem.' The message is the same. There can be no lasting peace in the Middle East without a road map for justice and peace in Israel and Palestine.

After several courtesy calls to church leaders, and a splendid lunch at the Armenian Patriarchate, we began the journey home from Tel Aviv.

Saying our farewells at Heathrow underlined the personal and long-lasting benefits of the pilgrimage. Friendships have been deepened, ecumenical confidence strengthened, and we have proved it is possible for Church leaders to act and speak with one voice on a global issue.

As one of the party said: 'This pilgrimage was beyond excellent.'

Christmas Eve

At 6.30 a.m. my mind was focused on the live interview for the BBC Radio 4 *Sunday* programme at 7:45 and Rob Frost had also asked if I would speak with him on his Premier

Radio breakfast show. In-between, I was downloading some photos that I could show during the morning service at Didcot Baptist Church. Interspersed into all this was a sense of relief that I had completed my Christmas shopping before the visit to Bethlehem!

Before I entered the Christmas celebrations with the family, I listed my final reflections:

1. I am still processing the deep emotions that overwhelmed me on a number of occasions. The despair at the humanitarian crisis; the anger at the manifest injustices; the frustration at the apparent lack of will to seek any viable political solution; the sadness for the apparent exclusion of the evangelical churches from the regular meetings of church leaders.

2. I am making the private pledge that my global ministry will fulfil the promise to be a voice for the voiceless and speak up for the people of Bethlehem. If the Palestinian Christian family feels isolated, then we need to respond to their request: Pray for Israel *and* pray for Palestine.

3. The fellowship between the four presidents has been memorable. The level of trust and confidence and open sharing has gone beyond anything we have experienced in our quarterly meetings. We have discussed one or two initiatives we can take together that will make a significant contribution. We now need to make firm decisions on these initiatives.

4. There are good interfaith relations here in the UK, especially in the Council of Christians and Jews and

the Christian Muslim Forum. The role of the Jewish-Christian-Muslim leaders in Jerusalem is unique, and we should be asking what the UK faith leaders can do to strengthen the contribution of the faith leaders of the Holy Land.

5. The stories of hope must be shared. We met people with inspiring vision on both sides of the conflict and their voices deserve to be heard. The parable of Mitri Raheb's olive tree is one that remains. His message is: 'If we don't plant any trees today, there will be nothing tomorrow. But if we plant a tree today, there will be shade for the children to play in, there will be oil to heal the wounds, and there will be olive branches to wave when peace arrives.'[93]

93. Raheb, *Bethlehem Besieged*, p. 157.

Her Majesty Queen Elizabeth died at Balmoral Castle on 8 September 2022.

After days of public mourning, her funeral service was held at Westminster Abbey on Monday, 19 September.

I was invited to contribute this article to the online edition of Baptist Times. It was also published in Premier Christianity online. It is reproduced with permission.[94]

---

94. Edited for the purposes of this book.

23

Personal Memories of
Her Majesty Queen Elizabeth II

I had the privilege of meeting Her Majesty Queen Elizabeth II, and many times observing her on duty on national occasions. My first meeting was in July 1986 at a Buckingham Palace garden party. I had been inducted as president of the Baptist Union at the end of April that year.

In May, I was a member of the ecumenical delegation of British church leaders that visited the Soviet Union. Mikhail Gorbachev assumed his leadership in 1985, and the process of *glasnost* and *perestroika* had begun.

My wife, Janet, and I had no idea in advance that we would meet any royal family member, let alone the Queen. Randomly, guests at the garden party were approached by Lord Airlie, the Lord Chamberlain and invited to stand to one side to greet the Queen. My wife and I were among the guests selected and minutes later found ourselves in conversation with the Queen.

Her Majesty was keenly interested to learn of my recent visit to the Soviet Union. I was able to share that, while standing in Red Square, a group of older Russian women discovered we were from the United Kingdom and immediately exclaimed: 'We love your Queen and the royal family!' We worked out these older women would have been ten years of age when the Russian royal family were brutally assassinated in 1918. The Queen commented on her Russian relatives and said she had never visited the Soviet Union but would love that opportunity one day. Eight years later, she did make a State visit to Russia, in October 1994, the first ruling British monarch to set foot on Russian soil.

The months of March and April at Windsor Castle used to be known as Easter Court. During this time, the Queen and the Duke of Edinburgh would host 'dine and sleep' events at the castle. Guests arrived early evening, enjoyed an evening meal, slept overnight at the castle and left after breakfast. Janet and I were privileged to receive an invitation to a 'dine and sleep' event in April 1995. Unfortunately, the fire of 1992 meant no sleepover accommodation at Windsor Castle. Still, we could enjoy an informal evening dinner with the royal couple and their fourteen guests. It was so relaxed there were corgis under the table throughout the meal hoping for scraps to fall. The provost of Oriel College, Oxford and his wife were guests, and the Queen was amused we didn't know each other and hadn't travelled together from Oxford!

After dinner, we were taken to the Grand Corridor, where individual items were displayed on tables. They had been selected for each guest from the Windsor Castle library and were personal to our life and background. Our first item was a handwritten note from Queen Victoria to William Gladstone. She requested her Prime Minister: 'To be kind to the nonconformists among us as they do us good.' The second item was a photograph of a young

Charles Haddon Spurgeon with his wife, Susannah. I hadn't seen this particular portrait of Spurgeon and his wife, and it was impressive to discover the library staff had carefully researched my ministry background. As each guest looked at their items, the Queen and Duke came alongside to see our reactions. I confess I was more knowledgeable in commenting on Spurgeon than Gladstone and, with prior notice, would have recalled the attitude of veneration that nineteenth-century nonconformists held for Gladstone.

My third memory of Her Majesty the Queen was one of observation while attending a service in Westminster Abbey in October 1995. I was one of the ecumenical guests at the opening service for the Sixth General Synod of the Church of England. The preacher was the Rev Dr Oliver O'Donovan, whose sermon theme was the importance of speech to the Christian faith.

He urged members of Synod not to be hustled by deadlines, panic or someone's urgent advocacy. It could have been a message designed to encourage this Baptist pastor.

The service concluded with communion. As the Queen came forward and knelt to receive the bread and wine from the archbishop, the choir were singing a beautiful anthem about the presence of God. I found the image of the kneeling monarch very poignant, as a few days earlier Princess Diana had given her now infamous BBC *Panorama* interview to Martin Bashir where she spoke candidly about her broken marriage relationship. Twenty-three million viewers viewed the programme, and the worldwide audience was estimated to be 200 million across 100 countries.

That morning in the Abbey, I saw a woman of faith kneeling in prayer, her hands opened to receive the bread and wine, symbolising the spiritual needs of one family needing God's grace during a public crisis. In many of the public tributes to the Queen, her strong Christian faith has been emphasised, supported by the words of her personal testimony in her Christmas Day message in 2014:

> For me the life of Jesus Christ, the Prince of Peace . . . is an inspiration and an anchor in my life. A role-model of reconciliation and forgiveness, he stretched out his hands in love, acceptance and healing. Christ's example has taught me to seek to respect and value all people of whatever faith and none.[95]

---

95. Mark Greene, *A Life of Grace: A Tribute to Queen Elizabeth II* (Swindon: Bible Society, HOPE Together, LICC 2022), p. 51.

Epilogue

Plymouth Sound 2016

'Growing Old With God' was a sermon preached at Upton Vale in January 2016. There used to be an afternoon service once a month called 'Songs of Praise'. It attracted an older congregation who loved to sing familiar hymns and enjoyed catching up with old friends. I was seventy-five when I preached on this passage, but editing it in my eighty-second year, the truths contained in Psalm 71 are even more meaningful.

24

Growing Old with God

Psalm 71

An elderly woman was interviewed on her 105th birthday and asked if she had any worries or anxieties. She replied, 'I have no worries or anxieties since I got my son into an old people's home.'[96]

I'm not ready just yet for an old people's home but it's a sign you are getting older when your Christmas present from your younger brother is an annual subscription to the *Oldie* magazine! The magazine has been described as a haven for grumpy old men and women. It offers no advice on retirement or growing old, just a steady stream of good sense, wit and entertainment. Thus far I've read two editions and not discovered anything I did not know already about ageing.

There are two wrong ways to growing old and they are reflected in our culture. The first is the fruitless quest for eternal youth. There are studies exploring the possibilities

---

96. Source unknown.

of physical immortality. Major advances in medical science promise future generations a life free from ageing, and in reputable journals you can read the wild predictions that future generations will defeat death itself.

The second wrong way of approaching old age is succumbing to the condition known as Geraphobia – which is the fear of growing old. It is marked by an anxiety about declining physical powers. Geraphobia is being concerned at the onset of irritability.

I never used to shout at the television when I was in my twenties.
I was never impatient in my thirties queuing at the supermarket.
In my forties I never went upstairs,
having to return downstairs to remember why
I had gone upstairs in the first place!

The biblical response to the onset of geraphobia is claiming God's promise of a fruitful old age. He says he will not abandon us when we grow old. The psalmist asks God to make him fruitful in his old age. He says he wants to 'flourish [spiritually] like a palm tree' and grow tall like a cedar tree in the house of the Lord. He desires to 'bear fruit in [his] old age', 'fresh and green' and full of life - proclaiming the Lord's goodness (Psalm 92:12-15). There is no hint of geraphobia here. This is embracing the last years of life with a spiritual zeal.

Psalm 71 is suggested as *the* psalm for growing old with God. It was written by an old believer, possibly David or Jeremiah in their old age. The writer has a long memory of God's faithfulness.

He ponders on walking with God through many years.
He has built a storehouse of wisdom.
He can testify that every day there have been new
mercies.
Each day he can say: 'God has been faithful to me.'

A helpful way of looking at this psalm is to see what is said
about yesterday, today and tomorrow.

The psalmist begins by *looking back with thanksgiving.*
He realises that from the moment he was born he has
relied on the Sovereign Lord, who 'brought me forth from
my mother's womb' (v. 6). Since his youth the Lord has
been his hope and confidence and the one who has taught
him (vv. 5,17).

At some point in our journey through life we should
reflect gratefully on God's goodness to us in our birth and
childhood and growing years. Whatever the circumstances
of our earliest years, whether they were filled with love
and care or cruelty and lovelessness, we are invited to
consider where the Lord has been 'a rock of refuge, to
which I can always go' (v. 3). I know some people who have
a storehouse of shame and sadness from their youngest
years, and they read verse 6 like this:

From my birth I had to rely on you, Lord,
because I realise there was nothing humanly reliable
in my life
from the day I was born.
And I am only alive today because of your loving care.

If you are brave enough, look back to yesterday and
open the doors of the house called 'memory' you have
not visited in years and be prepared for the holes in your

heart to be mended. John Claypool, in his book *Mending the Heart*, shares the story of looking back on his life. He was angry with his ageing mother for her domineering tendencies, until it dawned on him that her imperfections had not originated with her at all. For some reason he had never given any thought to his mother's past. As he began to think about her mother and her grandmother and even her great-grandmother, he says: 'I realised that the wounds she had inflicted on me had grown, at least in part, from the wounds that had been inflicted on her. With that perception, a log jam of hostility broke free in me that day: I could perceive my mother differently – with more compassion and mercy – by seeing her against the background of her own history.' [97]

It is possible, with God's help, to look back with thanksgiving on our past and seek his healing grace to mend the holes in our hearts.

The second thing the psalm teaches us about ageing is to *look around with hope*. Last autumn Janet and I attended a day conference for retired ministers and missionaries, and we listened to an inspiring talk by a retired doctor living in Exeter. He shared the story of a friend who, following his retirement, had taken a part-time job working with B&Q. His contract required him to commence work at 9 a.m. each morning, but he was consistently late, often arriving ten minutes after the hour. After a few days, the manager had to challenge him about his late arrival at work and asked him why he was not punctual when he was paid to be on duty at 9 a.m. He said, 'You were in the navy for many years, what did your senior officers say when you arrived late for work?' The man replied, 'They would say:

---

97. John Claypool, *Mending the Heart* (Boston, MA: Cowley Publications, 1999), p. 13.

"Good morning, Admiral. Will it be tea or coffee today?"' That's what I call living life with a hope-filled attitude!

As the psalmist considers his life, he reflects on the troubles he has experienced which he describes as 'many and bitter' (v. 20). One of the advantages of your older years is you have a long memory of God's faithfulness. You can recall numerous occasions when God brought you through difficult days; the times when God delivered you from the many and bitter experiences you endured. The psalmist has his personal moments of God rescuing him stored in his memory – but even in old age he needs that divine deliverance again. Something has arisen in his life. We don't know what situation he is describing. All we possess is the language of a deep descent into the depths.

Was the writer:

Sinking in sorrow?
Drowning in despair?
Buried in bereavement?

He is so low in the depths of the earth he probably fears he might sink without trace. But then he remembers the past occasions when God has rescued him. He realises, however low he is sinking in sorrow and despair, the Lord has fixed a limit to the descent into the depths and there will come a moment of resurrection. Because God always knows a way out of the deadly depths of a grave. This fills the psalmist with hope, and he exclaims: 'You will restore my life again; from the depths of the earth you will again bring me up' (v. 20). There is a hint that the writer may have been disgraced and shamed by the experience he has passed through. He has a revived confidence regarding his damaged reputation as he testifies: 'You will increase my honour and comfort me once more' (v. 21).

Jonathan Aitken is someone who knows what it is to be publicly shamed and disgraced. He was an MP who served as a cabinet minister and held the post of chief secretary to the Treasury. But in 1999 his world fell apart when he was caught telling a lie while under oath. He was convicted at the Old Bailey of perverting the course of justice and perjury and sentenced to eighteen months in prison. He had already experienced divorce, and now there was disgrace and bankruptcy. He was trapped in the depths with no apparent way of escape. In his book, *Psalms for People under Pressure*, he describes how, prior to being sentenced at the Old Bailey, a friend gave him a copy of a booklet on the Psalms and on his first night in prison, he turned to the passage for that day which was Psalm 130 and read:

Out of the depths I cry to you, O LORD;
O Lord, hear my voice.
Let your ears be attentive
to my cry for mercy.[98]

Aitken says he read the eight short verses of this psalm, 'and a warm and comforting wave of reassurance flooded over me. Suddenly I realised I was not as lonely, scared, helpless or vulnerable as I thought.'[99] The words of the psalm spoke to him with such reassurance that he prayed over it every single day of his imprisonment, sometimes sharing it with his fellow inmates. He says how other prisoners joined him in reading the psalms, In prison parlance there was: 'a blagger (armed robber), a dipper (pickpocket), kiter (fraudster) and lifer (murderer).'[100]

---

98. NIV 1984.
99. Jonathan Aitken, *Psalms for People Under Pressure* (London: Continuum, 2004), p. xii.
100. Ibid., p. xv.

Whatever time of life, but especially in old age, there are no depths where God cannot come to us in his resurrection power. Share in the confident faith of the writer and say to the Lord:

You will restore my life again;
from the depths of the earth
you will again bring me up.
(v. 20)

The final encouragement for growing old with God is to *look forward with a vision.*

I love the energy of verse 18: 'Even when I am old and grey, do not forsake me, my God'. Was this a selfish prayer? No! Read further and discover why he was making this request. He was asking the Lord not to desert him because he wanted to declare God's power to the next generation. He was eager for the next generation to discover the might of the Lord in their own lives.

There are verses in this psalm which reveal an old believer who is bursting to share their testimony to God's goodness. Just look at the list:

My mouth is filled with your praise (v. 8).
As for me, I shall always have hope (v. 14).
I will praise you more and more (v. 14).
My mouth will tell of your righteous deeds (v. 15).
I will . . . proclaim your mighty acts (v. 16).
I will proclaim your righteous deeds, yours alone (v. 16).
My lips will shout for joy (v. 23).
My tongue will tell of your righteous acts all day long (v. 24).

I love the 'more and more'! This aged believer is not slowing down. He is burning to share his story of God's goodness with others. His vision is looking forward with the years left to sharing his testimony.

There is a prevailing mood in some church circles that if you are over sixty there is no place for you to serve in the church family. Some are concerned that if you present the image of an ageing church to the wider world then younger people won't be attracted to join your fellowship.

The biblical story presents an alternative scenario. Check out the opening chapters of Luke's Gospel and it is older believers who play a major role in the Nativity story. Where would we be without Elizabeth and Zechariah, the aged parents of John the Baptist; Simeon, the old man who was given the promise from God that he wouldn't die until he saw the Messiah; Anna, the prophetess, who was so full of spiritual vigour at the age of eighty-four that she never left the Temple but worshipped night and day, fasting and praying (Luke 1:5-25; Luke 2:21-38)?

Every church fellowship needs spiritual grandparents who, from their storehouse of spiritual memories, can share their wisdom of walking with God for many years. I recall with thanksgiving the numerous occasions when an older believer lifted the spirit of a prayer meeting with a discerning prayer; offered calm words of wisdom which released a logjam of confusion at a church meeting; delivered a timely word of encouragement which refreshed the hearts of the saints.

A few years ago, I conducted the funeral of Violet Agnes Mason, a retired missionary, aged ninety-two. Vee, as she was known, was born in Plymouth in 1922 and when she left school, her first job was as a shorthand typist for the Western National Omnibus Company. Then Vee trained at Charing Cross Hospital and gained her SRN and SCM[101] qualifications.

After the Second World War, Vee heard the call to overseas service and was accepted as a missionary by the Baptist Missionary Society (BMS) in 1951. After language training she sailed for the Belgian Congo in October 1952. She was twenty-three days at sea and then faced a long arduous road journey to the jungle hospital at Bolobo where she would serve as a nurse.

The greatest challenge of her life occurred in 1964. The 1960s was a period of turbulent political change in the Congo. When independence came in June 1960, within a week the Congolese army had mutinied against the white Belgian officers and fighting broke out between Congolese and Belgian troops. In parts of the Congo the unrest assumed a specifically anti-white hatred, and in the south of the country some of the missionaries were severely beaten and raped.

The BMS decided to evacuate some of its missionaries, but Vee was among those who stayed. The United Nations forces remained in the country as peacemakers for three years, but they left in June 1963. Within a year another rebellion had broken out and from August 1964 more than eighty Europeans were murdered, including Protestant and Catholic missionaries.

The town of Bolobo was captured by rebel soldiers and for a few weeks the missionaries were under house arrest. Rebel soldiers allowed Bolobo hospital to continue to function, but eventually government troops recaptured Bolobo and, after a short battle, soldiers then surrounded the hospital. All the staff were made to lie on the ground

---

101.State Registered Nurse and State Certificate in Midwifery.

with guns at their necks while they checked there were no rebels hiding in the hospital grounds. It was a tricky moment for the medical staff including Vee, and a decision was taken to evacuate most of the missionaries. BMS left four missionaries in post to keep the hospital functioning and Vee was one of that group of four.[102]

Vee loved the words of Psalm 121 and during those dangerous days she found this scripture sustained her faith:

The LORD will keep you from all harm –
he will watch over your life;
the LORD will watch over your coming and going
both now and for evermore.
(Psalm 121:7-8)

By the time I met Vee she had been retired for many years. She was in her mid-eighties, frail and nearly blind. She was a faithful attender at church services until her final months. The highlight of her later years was an annual visit to the Youth Bible Class on a Sunday morning. The youth leaders invited an ageing Vee to tell the story I have just shared with you. They wanted a younger generation to hear Vee's story of courage and endurance, and how the Lord had protected her living in a dangerous war zone.

Vee's medical knowledge was out-of-date, and she would never survive twenty-three days at sea. Physically she was blind and frail. But she could read the psalm we have been considering and testify boldly to the young people in the Bible class:

---

102. I am grateful to Angus MacNeill for providing me with this first-hand account. He and his wife, Carol, were part of the small missionary contingent who remained at Bolobo hospital.

Since my youth the Lord has taught me.
Today I can share the wonderful things he did through my life.
Now I am old and grey and almost blind,
I ask the Lord never to forsake me
because I want to declare his power to the next generation.
(based on Psalm 71:17-18)

If you want to make the most of the rest of your life and fulfil God's promise of spiritual fruitfulness in old age, then follow Vee and grow old with God.

Acknowledgements

Thank you to Martin Brace, who encouraged me to produce in writing some of my sermons. He was so passionate about this conviction that he drove to my house one morning with a scribbled note of what the Lord had said to him in his devotions about my producing a book. God used Martin to convince me to start the journey.

My book club companions, Andrew Green and Dave Hewitt, have been a constant resource of shared wisdom and pastoral encouragement. I am grateful to David Scott, journalist, author and proud fan of Burnley FC, who has regularly offered his ideas about the best ways to bring a book to the marketplace.

Thank you to Mary Parker, my friend and colleague from the Baptist Union. She was the first to till the ground of my early manuscript and offered me the best encouragement by saying she had been spiritually blessed by reading the book.

I owe a massive debt to friends of sixty years, Phil and Mary Greenslade. Phil and I were students at Spurgeon's College. I am grateful to them for reading the draft of my book more than once. Daily, they sent emails packed with suggestions, questions and humorous asides. Their library collection is unique, and they deserve the accolade of exceptional bibliophiles.

I express my appreciation to my publisher, Malcolm Down, for his warm encouragement, and advice and to my copy editor, Sheila Jacobs, who improved the text considerably with her forensic eye for detail.

Finally, thank you to my wife and best friend, Janet Anne. I first saw her in a crowded school playground when she was fourteen. For me, it was love at first sight. But Janet has never returned the compliment by saying she loved me when she first saw me. She says she grew to love me because I played the piano and made her laugh. My piano-playing days are fewer, but there is humour and laughter every day. Our friendship has deepened and broadened in retirement. The best hour of the day is enjoying an early morning cup of tea, reading the Scriptures aloud together, and interceding for family, friends and the world God loves. I don't share Janet's love for cryptic crosswords, but then she doesn't delight in the poetry of George Herbert.

Almost every event alluded to in this book I have shared with Janet. When she read the early drafts of the manuscript, she spotted the exaggerations, and I soon discarded them. She observed the foggy logic, and after my modest defence, I rewrote a paragraph. She was endlessly patient with the slow gestation of the promised volume and occasionally said, 'Come out of your study and join me in the garden.'

We both know the word 'forever' can never apply to a loving marriage friendship, however long it endures (fifty-seven years and counting). So I accept the advice of James Runcie who, in the closing words of his moving memoir to his late wife, Marilyn, says to the reader:

Seize the day, remember well, love fiercely.[103]

---

103. James Runcie, *Tell Me Good Things: On Love Death and Marriage* (London: Bloomsbury Publishing, 2022), p. 208.